What's the Difference?
ANIMALS

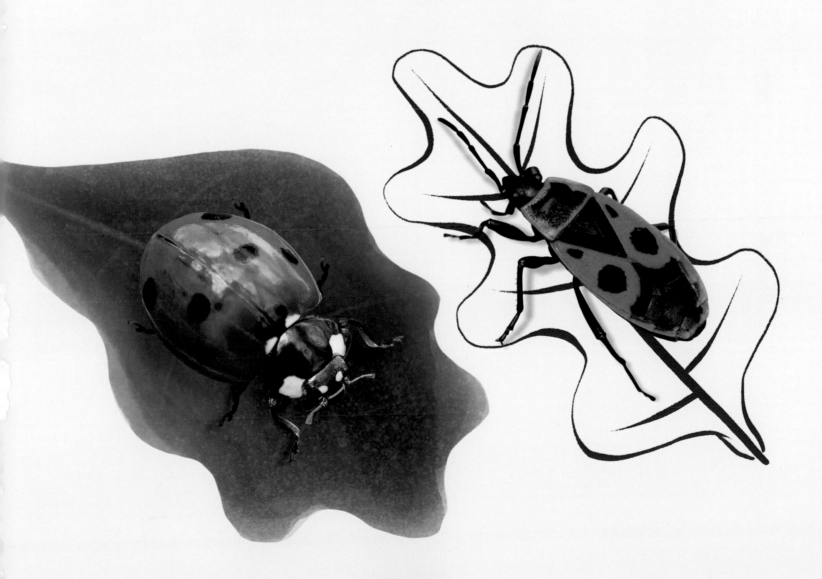

Penguin Random House

Author Susie Rae
Consultant Nick Crumpton
Illustrator Dilbag Singh

Senior editors Satu Fox, Roohi Sehgal
Project art editors Polly Appleton, Kanika Kalra

Project editor Manisha Majithia
Art editors Sadie Thomas, Bhagyashree Nayak
Additional design Nidhi Mehra
US editor Margaret Parrish
US Senior editor Shannon Beatty
Jacket designers Polly Appleton, Kanika Kalra
Project picture researcher Sakshi Saluja
Production editor Dragana Puvacic
Production controller Magdalena Bojko
DTP designers Sachin Gupta, Satish Gaur
Acquisitions editor Fay Evans
Managing editors Penny Smith, Monica Saigal
Managing art editor Ivy Sengupta
Publishing coordinator Issy Walsh
Delhi creative heads Glenda Fernandes,
Malavika Talukder
Deputy art director Mabel Chan
Publishing director Sarah Larter

First American edition, 2022
Published in the United States by DK Publishing
1450 Broadway, Suite 801, New York, NY 10018

A catalog record for this book
is available from the Library of Congress.
ISBN 978-0-7440-5658-7

DK books are available at special discounts when purchased
in bulk for sales promotions, premiums, fund-raising, or educational
use. For details, contact: DK Publishing Special Markets,
1450 Broadway, Suite 801, New York, NY 10018
SpecialSales@dk.com

Printed and bound in China

For the curious
www.dk.com

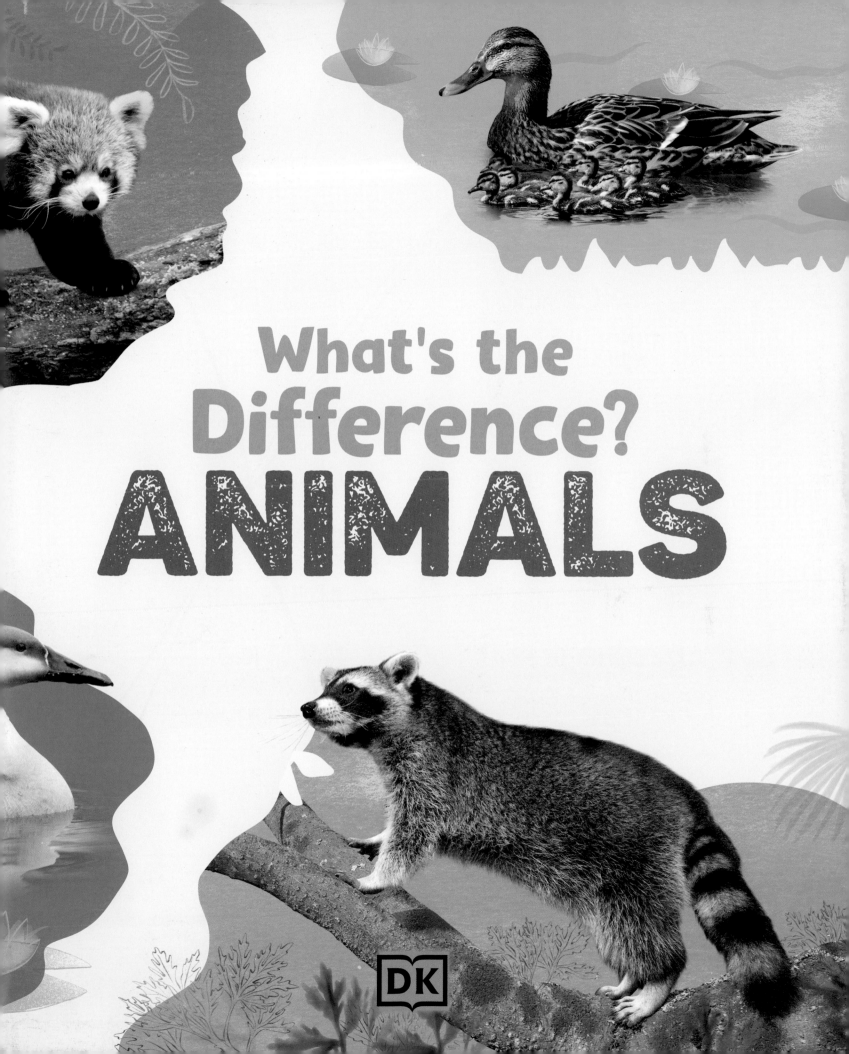

What's the Difference? ANIMALS

DK

CONTENTS

Common kestrel

Red-tailed hawk

WHO'S WHO?

Animals come in all shapes and sizes. Lots of things affect how animals look—including where they live, what they eat, and whether they fly, run, or swim. Animals with the same features belong to a species. A species is part of a family group in which the animals are similar but not the same. For example, coyotes and jackals are two species that belong to the dog family.

Mountain coyote

Golden jackal

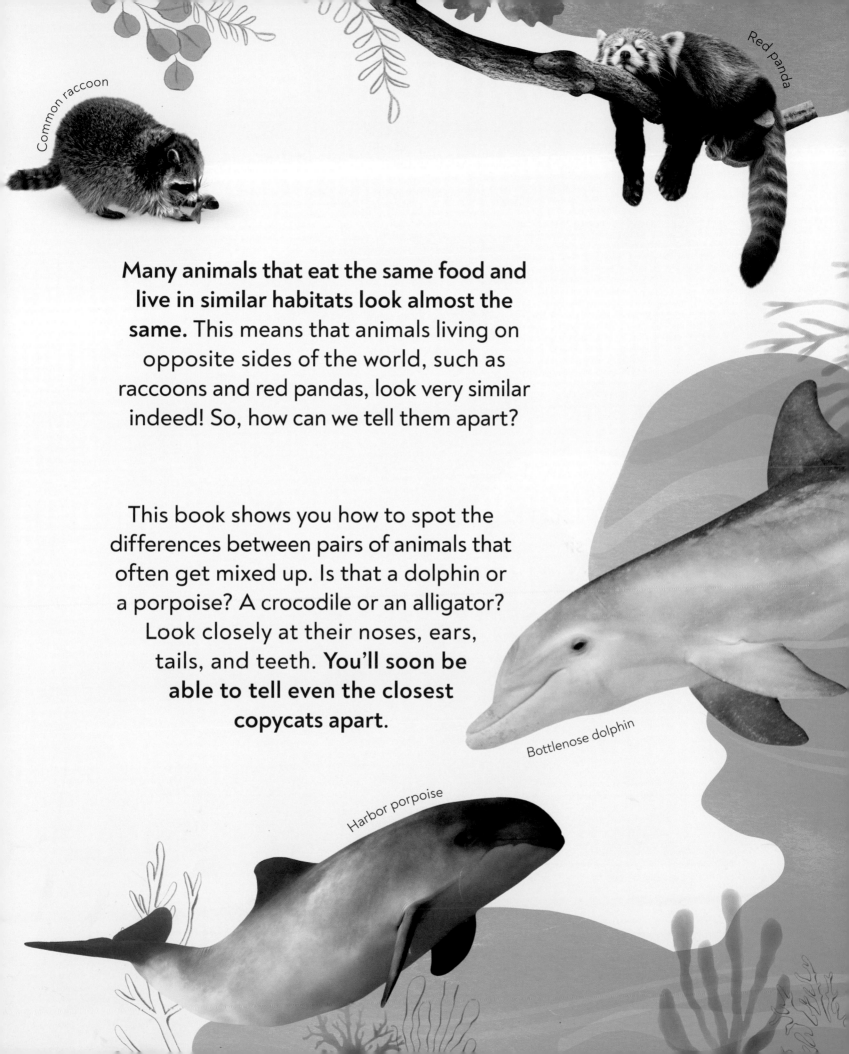

Common raccoon

Red panda

Many animals that eat the same food and live in similar habitats look almost the same. This means that animals living on opposite sides of the world, such as raccoons and red pandas, look very similar indeed! So, how can we tell them apart?

This book shows you how to spot the differences between pairs of animals that often get mixed up. Is that a dolphin or a porpoise? A crocodile or an alligator? Look closely at their noses, ears, tails, and teeth. You'll soon be able to tell even the closest copycats apart.

Bottlenose dolphin

Harbor porpoise

CROCODILE OR ALLIGATOR?

Crocodiles and alligators are big reptiles with strong teeth and jaws. They both like to spend their days lazing around in the water. But look closer, and you'll spot some important differences.

Scales can be different shades of gray, green, brown, or black

BOTH CAN STAY UNDERWATER FOR MORE THAN AN HOUR

Long, pointed snout

Bottom teeth show even when mouth is closed

AMERICAN CROCODILE

FAMILY RESEMBLANCE?

Gharials are from the same family of reptiles as crocodiles and alligators. They have long, thin snouts, which they use to catch fish.

CROCODILE

ALLIGATOR

NAME
American crocodile

WHERE DO THEY LIVE?
Saltwater coasts, rivers, and lakes across Florida, Central and South America, and the Caribbean

HOW BIG ARE THEY?
8½–15 ft (2.5–4.5 m) long

WHAT DO THEY EAT?
Almost anything: birds, fish, turtles, dogs, goats, and sharks

NAME
American alligator

WHERE DO THEY LIVE?
Freshwater rivers and swamps in southeastern United States

HOW BIG ARE THEY?
8½–11 ft (2.5–3.4 m) long

WHAT DO THEY EAT?
Small prey, such as birds, frogs, fish, and snails, as well as larger mammals, such as rabbits

NOW YOU KNOW!

Look at their heads. A crocodile's snout is long and pointed, while an alligator's is wide and curved. Are their teeth sticking out? That's a croc. Make sure you're looking from a safe distance!

BOTH ARE COLD-BLOODED, SO THEY HAVE TO WARM THEIR BODIES IN THE SUN

Wide, curved, U-shaped snout

Dark-colored scales, usually dark green or black

Bottom teeth mostly hidden when mouth is closed

AMERICAN ALLIGATOR

LLAMA OR ALPACA?

High up in the Andes mountains, in South America, live llamas and alpacas, cousins of the camel. Both of these animals are kept on farms, so that humans can turn their fur into wool for clothes and blankets. Watch out—they can spit when annoyed!

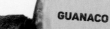

GUANACO

The guanaco is the llama's wild relative.

Long nose and not much hair on their face

NAME
Llama

WHERE DO THEY LIVE?
High plains of South America, and farms around the world

HOW BIG ARE THEY?
Around 47 in (120 cm) tall to the shoulder

WHAT DO THEY EAT?
Grass and other plants

NAME
Alpaca

WHERE DO THEY LIVE?
The Andes mountain range in South America, and farms across North and Central America

HOW BIG ARE THEY?
Around 35 in (90 cm) tall to the shoulder

WHAT DO THEY EAT?
Mostly grass and hay

Coarse, crinkly fur

LLAMAS WILL DEFEND THEIR HERD, INCLUDING OTHER ANIMALS, SUCH AS COWS, FROM PREDATORS

LLAMA

LLAMA **ALPACA**

Llamas are tall, confident animals with coarse fur, while alpacas are cute and cuddly with soft fur. Llamas and alpacas are close relatives and will often live together in the same herd.

VICUÑA

The vicuña is the alpaca's wild relative.

• Short, pointed ears

Furry, friendly-looking face with a blunt nose

Soft fur

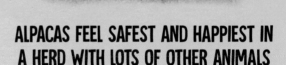

ALPACAS FEEL SAFEST AND HAPPIEST IN A HERD WITH LOTS OF OTHER ANIMALS

ALPACA

FAMILY RESEMBLANCE?

Alpacas and llamas, along with their wild relatives, are part of the camelidae family. The other animals in this group are dromedary camels (above) and bactrian camels, which both have humps.

FLOATING UPWARD
EAGLES HAVE LONG FEATHERS THAT GIVE THEM A VERY BROAD WINGSPAN. THEIR FEATHERS LET THEM GLIDE UPWARD ON WARM COLUMNS OF AIR, CALLED THERMALS.

BIRDS

Some birds fly fast and some hover in the air, some flap their wings hard, while others glide smoothly. This is because there are different types of wings, which work in different ways.

BALD EAGLE

HOVERING IN PLACE
SOME BIRDS FLAP THEIR WINGS VERY QUICKLY, WHICH LETS THEM HOVER IN PLACE AS THEY EAT OR LOOK FOR FOOD. THEIR TAILS HELP THEM TO STAY STABLE.

COMMON EUROPEAN KESTREL

BLACK-BROWED ALBATROSS

AIR ACROBATICS
THIS SHAPE IS PERFECT FOR SHORT BURSTS OF SPEED. BIRDS WITH ELLIPTICAL WINGS ARE VERY AGILE AND CAN CHANGE DIRECTION EASILY AS THEY FLY—SOME CAN EVEN DO SOMERSAULTS AND FLIPS MIDAIR!

RAVEN

LONG-DISTANCE TRAVELER
THIS LONG, NARROW WING SHAPE LETS BIRDS SOAR FOR LONG DISTANCES WITHOUT FLAPPING THEIR WINGS TOO MUCH. THESE WINGS NEED STRONG GUSTS TO RISE UP IN THE AIR.

Wings

Wings allow birds, insects, and even some mammals to soar through the air. They do this by pushing air underneath the flat surfaces of the wings, lifting them away from the ground. But are all wings the same?

MAMMALS

There is only one group of mammals that can fly—bats. Bat wings are actually long fingers, with thin skin stretched between them. Bats can move their "fingers" to change the shape of their wings.

COMMON SWIFT

HIGH SPEED

LONG, THIN WINGS ALLOW BIRDS TO FLY FAST AND STAY IN THE AIR FOR MONTHS AT A TIME. THESE WINGS ARE SMOOTH, SO AIR DOESN'T CATCH ON THE FEATHERS AND SLOW THE BIRD DOWN.

LIKE CROWS AND RAVENS WINGS, BAT WINGS ARE ELLIPTICAL WINGS, MEANING THEY CAN BE USED TO WEAVE AND DIVE THROUGH THE AIR WHILE BATS HUNT FOR FOOD.

BATS' WINGS HAVE CLAWS AT THE ENDS, SO THEY CAN USE THEM FOR CLIMBING TREES AS WELL AS FLYING.

FLYING FOX BAT

GLIDING, NOT FLYING!

Despite their name, flying squirrels don't actually fly. They have flaps of skin under their arms that let them glide through the air. This allows them to jump much farther and even change direction midair.

DRAGONFLY

INSECTS

Most insects have four wings. The front and back wings work together to lift the insect into the air. Some insects beat their wings so fast that human eyes can't see them moving!

HONEY BEE

LADYBIRD

Some birds have wings, but cannot fly!

FLIGHTLESS

OSTRICHES AND EMUS USE THEIR WINGS FOR BALANCE AS THEY RUN ON POWERFUL LEGS, WHILE PENGUINS USE THEIR WINGS LIKE FLIPPERS, TO PUSH THEMSELVES THROUGH THE WATER.

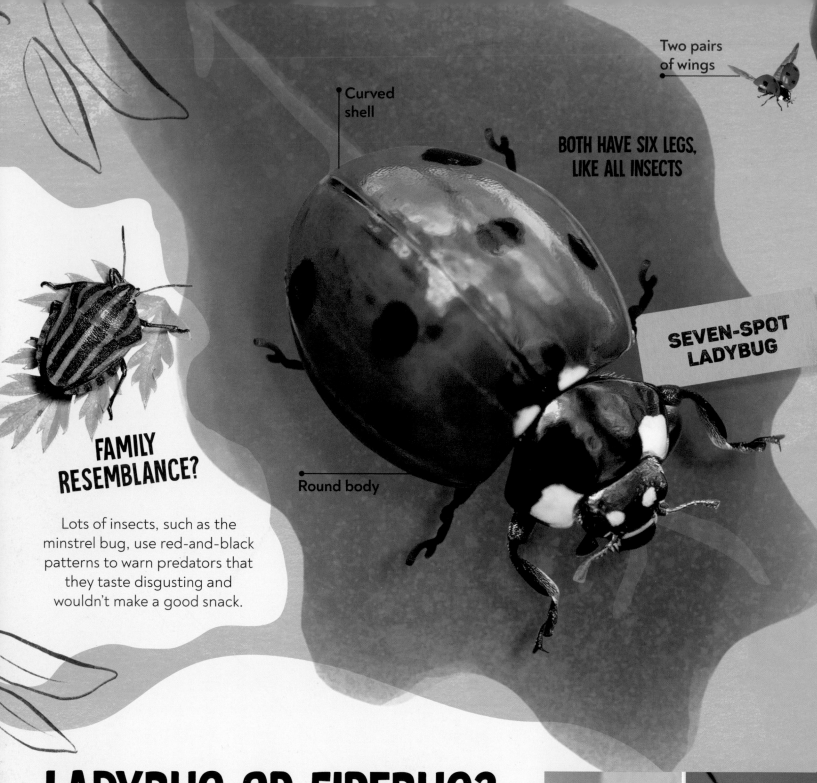

Curved shell

Two pairs of wings

BOTH HAVE SIX LEGS, LIKE ALL INSECTS

SEVEN-SPOT LADYBUG

Round body

FAMILY RESEMBLANCE?

Lots of insects, such as the minstrel bug, use red-and-black patterns to warn predators that they taste disgusting and wouldn't make a good snack.

LADYBUG OR FIREBUG?

What's that colorful insect? With their red-and-black spotted patterns, ladybugs and firebugs are easy to get mixed up. When you look past their spots, however, these bugs are very different.

LADYBUG

FIREBUG

NAME
Seven-spot ladybug

WHERE DO THEY LIVE?
Fields, meadows, gardens, and forests in Europe, North America, Asia, North Africa, and Australia

HOW BIG ARE THEY?
⅕–³⁄₁₀ in (5–8 mm)

WHAT DO THEY EAT?
Mostly tiny insects called aphids

NAME
Firebug

WHERE DO THEY LIVE?
Europe, China, Central America, India, and Australia

HOW BIG ARE THEY?
³⁄₁₀–⅖ in (8–10 mm)

WHAT DO THEY EAT?
Seeds

NOW YOU KNOW!

Look for their different body shapes to tell ladybugs and firebugs apart. The important thing about both of these pretty bugs is that, despite their colors, they're totally harmless!

Firebugs have tiny wings and can't fly

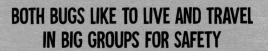

BOTH BUGS LIKE TO LIVE AND TRAVEL IN BIG GROUPS FOR SAFETY

A cluster of firebugs

Oval body

Flat shell

FIREBUG

15

BOTH EAT ALL SORTS OF FOOD, ALTHOUGH RED PANDAS PREFER BAMBOO

The main difference between red pandas and raccoons is their color. You can also look at their faces, ears, and hands for more clues, such as the raccoon's "eye mask."

Reddish-brown fur

Small, white eyebrows

Long, furry, ringed tail

Triangular ears

Paws with claws

RED PANDA

RED PANDA OR RACCOON?

With their thick, furry coats and long, striped tails, red pandas and raccoons look a lot alike. In fact, red pandas are more closely related to raccoons than giant pandas. Here are some differences to help you tell red pandas and raccoons apart.

RED PANDA

RACCOON

NAME
Red panda

WHERE DO THEY LIVE?
Mountainous forests in China and the Himalayas

HOW BIG ARE THEY?
20–25 in (50–64 cm) long, with a 11–23 in (28–60 cm) tail

WHAT DO THEY EAT?
Mostly bamboo, but also small mammals, birds, eggs, and berries

NAME
Common raccoon

WHERE DO THEY LIVE?
Forests, towns, and cities, mainly in North America, but also Europe and Japan

HOW BIG ARE THEY?
24–38 in (60–96 cm) long, with a 8–16 in (20–40 cm) tail

WHAT DO THEY EAT?
Almost anything, including plants, insects, eggs, frogs, and garbage left outside by humans

These young raccoons are fishing for crabs.

FAMILY RESEMBLANCE?

Native to Japan, tanuki are related to dogs and wolves. They look so much like raccoons that they're also called Japanese raccoon dogs.

Eye-mask markings

BOTH ARE AROUND THE SIZE OF A HOUSE CAT

Rounded ears

Black-and-white fur

Long, furry, ringed tail

Handlike paws with long fingers

COMMON RACCOON

SQUID OR OCTOPUS?

Dive under the ocean waves and you might find some squishy creatures with many limbs staring at you. They both have at least eight waving arms. How do you tell the difference between a squid and an octopus?

CARIBBEAN REEF SQUID

Caribbean reef squid have rounder bodies than most squid.

Eight arms with suckers

Round pupil

GIANT SQUID

Triangular head

Two feeding tentacles

NOW YOU KNOW!

Spot the difference by looking at the shape of a squid or octopus's head, or by checking their arms—both of them have eight arms with lots of suckers, but squid also have tentacles with suckers on the ends.

FAMILY RESEMBLANCE?

Cuttlefish are related to octopuses and squid but, unlike their squishy cousins, they have a hard, internal shell called a cuttlebone.

BOTH CAN CHANGE THE COLOR OF THEIR SKIN

SQUID

OCTOPUS

These tiny octopuses have a toxin that can even kill humans.

BLUE-RINGED OCTOPUS

BOTH ARE INVERTEBRATES, WHICH MEANS THEY DON'T HAVE A SKELETON

Round head

Rectangular pupil

GIANT PACIFIC OCTOPUS

NAME
Giant squid

WHERE DO THEY LIVE?
Deep in the world's oceans

LENGTH
40 ft (12 m) from head to the ends of their tentacles

WHAT DO THEY EAT?
Fish and other squid

NAME
Giant Pacific octopus

WHERE DO THEY LIVE?
The North Pacific Ocean

LENGTH
16 ft (5 m) from head to the ends of their arms

WHAT DO THEY EAT?
Smaller fish, shrimp, snails, clams, and sometimes other octopuses

Eight arms with suckers

EMU OR OSTRICH?

Emus and ostriches are the two biggest birds in the world. Even though they have fluffy feathers, neither can fly. Instead, both birds get away from trouble by running very fast. Can you tell which of these long-necked giants is which?

KIWI

The small, flightless kiwi lives in New Zealand.

FACT FILE

NAME
Emu

WHERE DO THEY LIVE?
Australia

HEIGHT
5–6 ft (1.5–1.9 m)

WHAT DO THEY EAT?
Plants and insects

NAME
Ostrich

WHERE DO THEY LIVE?
Native to North, East, and South Africa

HEIGHT
7–9 ft (2.1–2.8 m)

WHAT DO THEY EAT?
Plants, insects, and small reptiles

MALE EMUS KEEP THEIR EGGS WARM UNTIL THEY HATCH

EMU

Brown feathers

Three toes on each foot

20

NOW YOU KNOW!

Emus are the biggest animals in Australia, but they're small compared to ostriches. You can also tell the difference by looking at their feet—emus have three toes, while ostriches have two.

EMU

OSTRICH

MALE AND FEMALE OSTRICHES TAKE TURNS WARMING THEIR EGGS

Black-and-white feathers (males) or brown feathers (females)

Two toes on each foot

OSTRICH

FAMILY RESEMBLANCE?

The third-biggest bird in the world is the cassowary. It lives in Indonesia, Papua New Guinea, and parts of Australia.

DONKEY OR MULE?

There's a reason why donkeys and mules look so similar. Mules have a donkey father and a horse mother. A living thing that is a mix of different species is called a hybrid. So, how can you spot the differences between these close family members?

DONKEY

MULE

FAMILY RESEMBLANCE?

When a zebra and a donkey have a baby, it's called a zonkey!

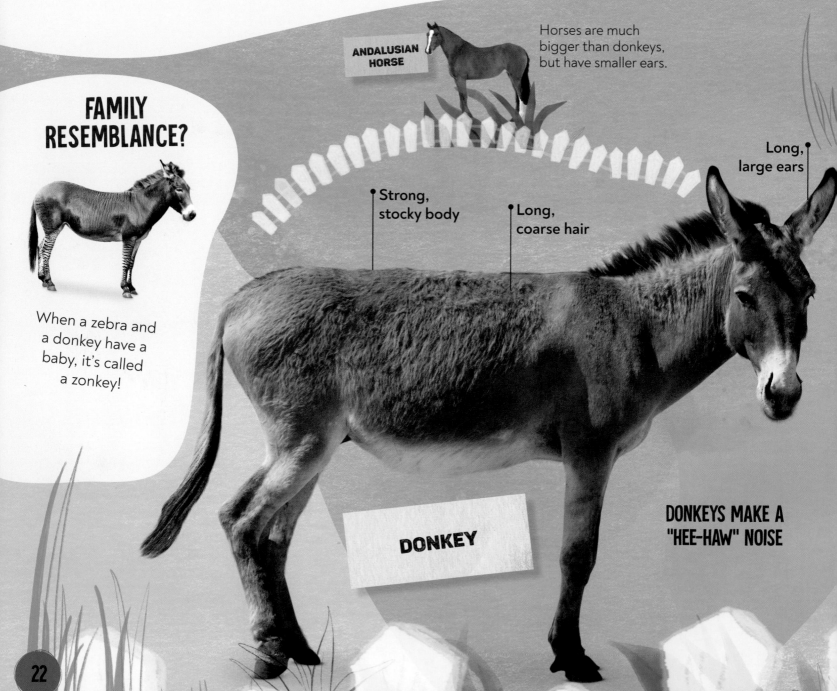

ANDALUSIAN HORSE

Horses are much bigger than donkeys, but have smaller ears.

Strong, stocky body

Long, coarse hair

Long, large ears

DONKEY

DONKEYS MAKE A "HEE-HAW" NOISE

NOW YOU KNOW!

There aren't many ways to tell mules apart from their donkey dads—except that they're a little bit horsier! Look at their hair and listen to the sound they make to see if you can tell the difference.

FACT FILE

NAME
Donkey

WHERE DO THEY LIVE?
All over the world, but especially China, Pakistan, and Ethiopia

HOW BIG ARE THEY?
3–5 ft (0.9–1.5 m) tall to the shoulder

WHAT DO THEY EAT?
Straw and grass

NAME
Mule

WHERE DO THEY LIVE?
All over the world, but especially China and Mexico

HOW BIG ARE THEY?
4–6 ft (1.2–1.8 m) tall to the shoulder

WHAT DO THEY EAT?
Hay and grain

Mules can have big donkey ears or smaller, horselike ears

PRZEWALSKI'S HORSE

This species is a wild horse that looks like a mule.

Short, smooth hair

Mules are strong like donkeys, but tend to be bigger

MULES MAKE A WHINNYING SOUND

MULE

CARNIVORES

Animals that eat other animals are called carnivores. They have sharp teeth for grabbing onto their prey. Their back teeth tend to be smaller, but they are still sharp enough to bite food into smaller chunks.

GREAT WHITE SHARK

BITING AND TEARING
MAMMAL CARNIVORES SUCH AS LIONS HAVE LONG, SHARP FRONT TEETH CALLED CANINES. A LIONS' CANINES ARE 4 IN (10 CM) LONG!

LAYERS OF SHARP TEETH
SHARKS HAVE MANY ROWS OF VERY SHARP TEETH THAT ARE ALL THE SAME SIZE. THEIR TEETH REGULARLY FALL OUT AND ARE REPLACED. THIS MEANS THEY ARE ALWAYS SHARP.

ASIATIC LION

TYPES OF TEETH

Incisors, the front teeth, are used for slicing. Canines, the pointed teeth beside the incisors, are sharp, for tearing meat. Premolars and molars, at the back, are big and flat, for crushing and chewing.

Teeth

Animals use their teeth not just for tearing, crunching, or chewing food, abut also for hunting and protecting themselves. You can tell a lot about an animal by the shape of its teeth.

HERBIVORES

Plant-eating mammals usually have sharp incisors at the front for biting and big molars at the back for grinding up their food.

STRONG NIBBLING TEETH
SQUIRRELS HAVE SHARP FRONT TEETH FOR BITING THROUGH HARD WOOD. THEIR TEETH ARE CONSTANTLY GROWING TO REPLACE PARTS THAT GET WORN DOWN BY GNAWING.

HIPPOPOTAMUS

BIGGEST CANINES
DESPITE BEING HERBIVORES, HIPPOPOTAMUSES HAVE THE ANIMAL KINGDOM'S LONGEST CANINES, AT 3 FT (1 M). THEY USE THESE TEETH TO PROTECT THEMSELVES.

SQUIRREL

POINTED PROTECTION
CHIMPANZEES EAT INSECTS AND PLANTS. THEY HAVE LONG CANINES TO DEFEND THEMSELVES FROM ATTACK, INCLUDING FROM OTHER CHIMPANZEES.

OMNIVORES

Animals that eat both meat and plants are called omnivores. They have broad, flat incisors for biting off chunks of food, sharp canines, and flat molars for chewing. Humans are omnivores!

PLANT-BASED BEAR
BLACK BEARS LOOK FEROCIOUS, BUT THEY MOSTLY USE THEIR TEETH FOR PULLING BERRIES OFF BRANCHES AND EATING GRASS.

CHIMPANZEE

BLACK BEAR

WORKING TOGETHER

GRAY WOLVES GRAB THEIR PREY WITH SHARP FRONT TEETH, THEN CUT IT INTO PIECES WITH THEIR BACK TEETH. SHEEP PULL UP PLANTS AND THEN GRIND THEM UP WITH THEIR BACK TEETH. BOTH ANIMALS HAVE THE RIGHT MIX OF TEETH FOR THE JOB.

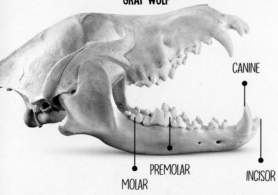

GRAY WOLF

CANINE

MOLAR

PREMOLAR

INCISOR

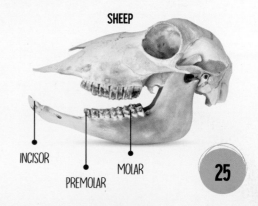

SHEEP

INCISOR

PREMOLAR

MOLAR

POSSUM OR OPOSSUM?

Known for scurrying around in cities and scavenging for their food, possums and opossums are very similar. Even their names are nearly the same! But if you look closely, there are lots of ways to tell these furry little marsupials apart.

POSSUM | OPOSSUM

Female possums usually give birth to, and take care of, just one baby.

BOTH LIVE NEAR HUMANS AND EAT THE TRASH WE THROW AWAY

Soft fur

Rounded face with brown eyes

FAMILY RESEMBLANCE?

Short-tailed opossums (below) are the size of mice. They live in the rain forests of South America but are also the perfect size to scurry into houses, where they eat pests such as insects and scorpions.

Furry, prehensile (grasping) tail

COMMON BRUSHTAIL POSSUM

NOW YOU KNOW!

You can tell which creature is digging through your garbage cans based on where you are—possums live in the southern hemisphere, opossums in the northern hemisphere. Their tails will also give you a clue!

Female opossums give birth to litters of around 20 young.

BOTH ARE MARSUPIALS, WHICH MEANS THEY CARRY THEIR BABIES IN A POUCH

Coarse fur

Pointed face with black eyes

Hairless tail

VIRGINIA OPOSSUM

DOLPHIN   **PORPOISE**

The Ganges river dolphin has pink skin rather than gray.

DOLPHINS ARE INTELLIGENT AND CURIOUS—THEY OFTEN APPROACH HUMANS

BOTTLENOSE DOLPHIN

Curved dorsal fin

Long body

DOLPHIN OR PORPOISE?

Dolphins and porpoises are cousins, part of a family called cetaceans. This family also includes whales. Although they live underwater, cetaceans are mammals, so they need to come to the surface to breathe. How can you tell these similar creatures apart?

NOW YOU KNOW!

Dolphins have long noses; porpoises have flatter ones. The shape of their fins are also different. You are more likely to spot a friendly dophin than a shy porpoise!

NAME
Bottlenose dolphin

WHERE DO THEY LIVE?
Oceans worldwide

HOW BIG ARE THEY?
6½–13 ft (2–4 m) long

WHAT DO THEY EAT?
Mostly fish, but also eels and squid

NAME
Harbor porpoise

WHERE DO THEY LIVE?
Cool waters in the North Atlantic and North Pacific Oceans

HOW BIG ARE THEY?
$4\frac{3}{5}$–$6\frac{1}{5}$ ft (1.4–1.9 m) long

WHAT DO THEY EAT?
Mostly fish, but also squid

DALL'S PORPOISE

Long, bottlelike "beak"

Black-and-white porpoises sometimes get mistaken for orcas.

Triangular dorsal fin

HARBOR PORPOISE

PORPOISES ARE SHY AND PREFER TO HIDE AWAY FROM PEOPLE

Rounded body

Short, stubby nose

FAMILY RESEMBLANCE?

Orcas are a kind of dolphin, the largest of the family. Like other dolphins, they are sociable and live in family groups called pods.

BEE OR WASP?

These small, yellow-and-black insects buzz by so quickly that it can be difficult to tell them apart! Both live in groups of thousands, both can sting when threatened, and both love to munch on flower nectar—but they have lots of differences, too.

BEE

WASP

FACT FILE

NAME
European honey bee

WHERE DO THEY LIVE?
Every continent except Antarctica

HOW BIG ARE THEY?
½–⅗ in (13–16 mm) long

WHAT DO THEY EAT?
"Bee bread," made from a mix of pollen and nectar

NAME
Eastern yellow jacket wasp

WHERE DO THEY LIVE
Eastern North America

HOW BIG ARE THEY?
½–⅗ in (13–16 mm) long

WHAT DO THEY EAT?
Dead insects, fruit, and nectar

Furry body

Fuzzy stripes

Round waist

Can only sting once

EUROPEAN HONEY BEE

BOTH ARE PROTECTIVE OF THEIR NESTS, WHERE THEIR QUEEN LIVES

The main difference between bees and wasps is their stripe pattern. Wasps have distinct bands, while bees' patterns are less clear. Bees are also furrier, to allow pollen to stick to them.

Smooth appearance

Narrow waist

These spindly wasps are easy to tell apart from bees.

ICHNEUMON WASP

Clear stripes

FAMILY RESEMBLANCE?

Bees and wasps are known for their yellow-and-black coloring. These colors let predators know that they sting. Some non-stinging insects, such as hoverflies, have similar colors to try and warn off attackers!

Can sting many times

EASTERN YELLOW JACKET WASP

RABBIT OR HARE?

These mammals are common sights on grasslands and can be found all over the world. But, although they both have long, furry ears, they are very different.

RABBIT

HARE

Pikas are mountain-dwelling relatives of rabbits and hares.

PIKAS

RABBITS LIVE IN UNDERGROUND BURROWS, CALLED WARRENS

Shorter ears

Live in groups

Short legs for hopping

EUROPEAN RABBIT

NOW YOU KNOW!

If you want to spot the difference between these animals, hares have longer legs and ears. Hares also live alone, above ground, while rabbit families burrow underground.

NAME
European rabbit

WHERE DO THEY LIVE?
Grasslands in Europe and parts of Australia

HOW BIG ARE THEY?
13–20 in (35–50 cm) long

WHAT DO THEY EAT?
Grass, fruit, and vegetables

NAME
Scrub hare

WHERE DO THEY LIVE?
Scrubland in southern Africa

HOW BIG ARE THEY?
18–26 in (44–65 cm) long

WHAT DO THEY EAT?
Mostly grass, but also leaves and tree bark

Longer ears

HARES CAN RUN AWAY FROM PREDATORS AT SPEEDS OF UP TO 40 MPH (65 KPH)

Male hares "boxing"

SCRUB HARE

Long hind legs for running

FAMILY RESEMBLANCE?

Some hares are adapted to cold environments. In the winter months, mountain hares' fur turns white so they can blend into the snow.

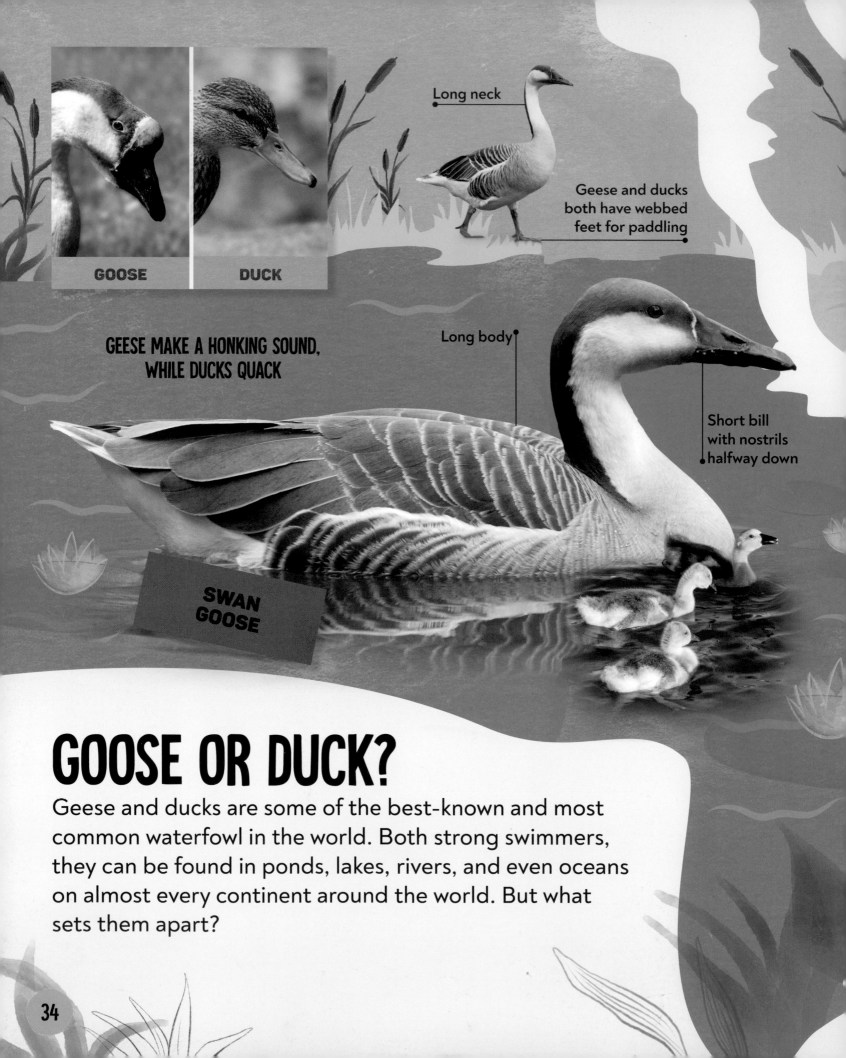

GOOSE

DUCK

Long neck

Geese and ducks both have webbed feet for paddling

GEESE MAKE A HONKING SOUND, WHILE DUCKS QUACK

Long body

Short bill with nostrils halfway down

SWAN GOOSE

GOOSE OR DUCK?

Geese and ducks are some of the best-known and most common waterfowl in the world. Both strong swimmers, they can be found in ponds, lakes, rivers, and even oceans on almost every continent around the world. But what sets them apart?

NOW YOU KNOW!

The main difference between these birds is size. Geese are generally bigger, with longer necks, while ducks have smaller, rounder bodies. Listen for their calls—if it quacks, it's a duck!

Male ducks are often more brightly colored than females

Short neck

Long bill with nostrils close to the eyes

Small, round body

BOTH FLY SOUTH IN THE WINTER TO FIND WARMER PLACES TO NEST

MALLARD DUCK

FAMILY RESEMBLANCE?

Swans are also water birds. They are known for their long necks and white feathers—although there are black swans in Australia.

FACT FILE

NAME
Swan goose

WHERE DO THEY LIVE?
Freshwater areas in Mongolia, China, and eastern Russia

HOW BIG ARE THEY?
31–37 in (81–94 cm) long

WHAT DO THEY EAT?
Water plants

NAME
Mallard duck

WHERE DO THEY LIVE?
Wetlands across every continent except Antarctica

HOW BIG ARE THEY?
20–26 in (50–65 cm) long

WHAT DO THEY EAT?
Slugs and snails, insects, worms, shellfish, and plants

EURASIAN LYNX

RHESUS MACAQUE

MAMMALS

Lots of mammals have claws, especially those that hunt prey. Claws can also be used to defend against attackers. Bears use their sharp claws to climb trees, while moles have long claws for digging. Monkeys and other primates use their claws for grooming.

ONLY WHEN NEEDED
CATS, SUCH AS LYNXES, HAVE RETRACTABLE CLAWS, WHICH THEY CAN PULL INSIDE THEIR PAWS WHEN THEY'RE NOT USING THEM.

Claws

Sharp nails, called claws, have lots of different uses, from catching prey and fighting, to climbing trees and digging. Claws come in handy for many different kinds of animals.

WHITE-TAILED EAGLE

BIRDS

Birds' claws are called talons. Birds of prey, including owls and eagles, swoop down and snatch up prey in their sharp talons. Birds use their talons for cleaning their feathers, gripping onto branches, carrying things around, and defending themselves.

GREEN IGUANA

WHAT ARE CLAWS MADE OF?

Most claws are made of keratin. This is the same material that makes up fingernails, horns, hooves, and even the hair on your head.

TIGHT GRIP
BIRDS OF PREY, SUCH AS EAGLES, HAVE FOUR CLAWS—THREE FACING FORWARD AND ONE FACING BACKWARD. THESE ALLOW THEM TO GRIP ONTO THEIR PREY.

TREE-DWELLER
IGUANAS SPEND MOST OF THEIR TIME IN THE TREETOPS OR BASKING IN THE SUN. THEIR LONG, CURVED CLAWS HELP THEM GRIP SO THEY DON'T FALL, EVEN WHEN ASLEEP.

REPTILES

Most reptiles have claws, even some snakes! Lizards use their claws for climbing and gripping. Reptiles that eat meat, from lizards to crocodiles, use their claws to catch and kill prey.

LEG BONES
BOA CONSTRICTORS HAVE TWO "CLAWS" POKING OUT TOWARD THE BACK OF THEIR BODIES. THESE ARE LEFT OVER FROM A TIME WHEN SNAKES HAD LEGS!

Snap, snap, snap!

CHRISTMAS ISLAND CRAB

CRABS AND LOBSTERS HAVE BIG CLAWS, CALLED PINCERS. THEY USE THEM TO CRUSH THE SHELLS OF PREY AND FIGHT OFF ATTACKERS. THEY EVEN "TALK" TO EACH OTHER BY RUBBING THEIR PINCERS TOGETHER.

Small, angular head

Long, slim body

Big, round spots

AFRICAN LEOPARD

BOTH PREFER TO LIVE ON THEIR OWN

LEOPARD OR JAGUAR?

These fierce creatures are both big, strong cats, with golden-brown, spotted fur. They prowl their habitats, hunting for large animals to bring down with their powerful jaws. These cat cousins look very similar at first. So what makes them different?

LEOPARD

JAGUAR

NOW YOU KNOW!

Leopards are smaller and less muscular than jaguars, but to tell the difference easily, look at their fur. Both cats have flower-shaped spots, but jaguars have smaller spots inside those.

FACT FILE

NAME
African leopard

WHERE DO THEY LIVE?
Desert, savanna, and rain forest in eastern and southern Africa

HOW BIG ARE THEY?
3–6¼ ft (90–190 cm) long, with a 2–3½ ft (60–110 cm) tail

WHAT DO THEY EAT?
Meat, including deer, snakes, and porcupines

NAME
Jaguar

WHERE DO THEY LIVE?
Forests and rain forests across Central and South America

HOW BIG ARE THEY?
5–6 ft (150–180 cm) long, with a 2–3 ft (60–90 cm) tail

WHAT DO THEY EAT?
Meat, including capybaras and deer

Big, round head

BOTH MAKE ROARING SOUNDS

Big spots with smaller spots inside them

Strong, stocky body

JAGUAR

FAMILY RESEMBLANCE?

Another similar-looking species of wild cat is the cheetah. This long, slender hunter can race across the savanna at up to 70 miles (112 km) an hour.

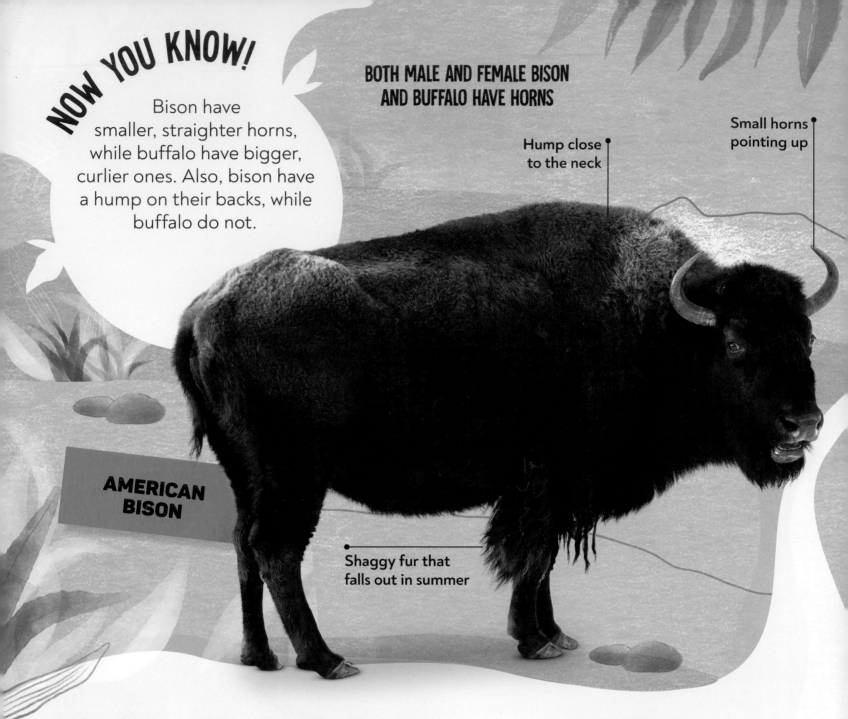

Bison have smaller, straighter horns, while buffalo have bigger, curlier ones. Also, bison have a hump on their backs, while buffalo do not.

BOTH MALE AND FEMALE BISON AND BUFFALO HAVE HORNS

Hump close to the neck

Small horns pointing up

AMERICAN BISON

Shaggy fur that falls out in summer

BISON OR BUFFALO?

Bison and buffalo are so easy to mix up that the word "buffalo" is often used to describe both animals. They're both related to cows, and they both have dark fur and horns. So, what differences can you notice between these creatures?

BISON

BUFFALO

NAME
American bison

WHERE DO THEY LIVE?
Prairies and plains
in North America

HOW BIG ARE THEY?
10 ft–11½ ft (3–3.5 m) long,
with a 1–3 ft (30–90 cm) tail

WHAT DO THEY EAT?
Mostly grass

NAME
Water buffalo

WHERE DO THEY LIVE
Near rivers and swamps
in India and Southeast Asia

HOW BIG ARE THEY?
8–10 ft (2.4–3 m) long, with a
2–3 ft (60–90 cm) tail

WHAT DO THEY EAT?
Water plants

BOTH LIVE IN BIG HERDS FOR PROTECTION

Big, curly
horns

Fur that stays
on all year round

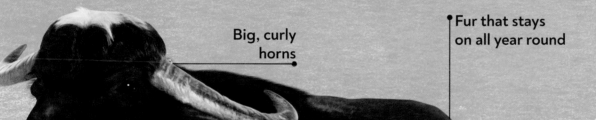

FAMILY RESEMBLANCE?

Most members of the cow
family have horns, which they
use for protection. Male yaks
(above) have big, curved
horns, while females have
smaller, straighter ones.

WATER BUFFALO

FROG OR TOAD?

Both of these little amphibians live in and near the water. They can swim and need lots of water to survive, but, unlike fish, they breathe using lungs. They can easily be spotted near freshwater almost anywhere in the world.

FROG   TOAD

NAME
Common frog

WHERE DO THEY LIVE?
Near ponds across Europe

HOW BIG ARE THEY?
3–5 in (8-13 cm) long

WHAT DO THEY EAT?
Insects, snails, slugs, and worms

NAME
Common toad

WHERE DO THEY LIVE?
Near deep ponds across Europe

HOW BIG ARE THEY?
3–5 in (8-13 cm) long

WHAT DO THEY EAT?
Insects, slugs, snails, worms, and small animals such as mice

Smooth, wet skin

Long body

COMMON FROG

Short legs

BOTH HAVE THREE TOES ON EACH FOOT

Frogs lay their eggs in clusters (above), while toads lay them in chains.

At first glance, frogs and toads seem almost identical, but they're very different. Look at their skin and legs to figure out which is which, or watch to see how they move. If it hops, it's a frog; if it crawls, it's a toad.

BOTH HAVE WIDE MOUTHS AND LARGE EYES

COMMON TOAD

Round body

MIDWIFE TOAD

Male midwife toads take care of their eggs until they are ready to hatch.

Bumpy, dry skin

Long legs

FAMILY RESEMBLANCE?

Salamanders are the lizardlike relatives of frogs and toads. Their skin has a dangerous toxin that stops animals from eating them.

FALCON OR HAWK?

Birds of prey are also called raptors. They feed on other animals, including other birds, which they grab with their sharp talons. Falcons, such as kestrels, and hawks both have impressive hunting skills and amazing eyesight, but they are very different birds.

Long, pointed wings

COMMON KESTREL

Small body

BOTH HAVE PALE FEATHERS WITH DARK SPOTS

FALCON   HAWK

44

NOW YOU KNOW!

The best way to tell a falcon, such as the kestrel, from a hawk is from the shape of their wings. Hawks glide on broad wings with jagged "fingers," while falcons flap their pointed wings hard to achieve superfast speeds.

BOTH HAVE SHARP TALONS FOR SNATCHING PREY

Wingtips look like fingers

RED-TAILED HAWK

Larger body

FAMILY RESEMBLANCE?

Eagles are the biggest birds of prey in the world after vultures. Eagles can see twice as far as humans—which is why we say someone is "eagle-eyed."

FACT FILE

NAME
Common kestrel

WHERE DO THEY LIVE?
A wide range of habitats across Europe, Africa, and Asia

HOW BIG ARE THEY?
12–15 in (32–39 cm) long, with a 25–32 in (65–82 cm) wingspan

WHAT DO THEY EAT?
Small mammals, such as mice and voles

NAME
Red-tailed hawk

WHERE DO THEY LIVE?
Mostly woodland habitats across North and Central America

HOW BIG ARE THEY?
18–26 in (45–65 cm) long, with a 2½–4½ ft (104–141 cm) wingspan

WHAT DO THEY EAT?
Any small animal, including rodents, fish, and frogs

SEAL OR SEA LION?

These water-loving mammals are a common sight on coastlines around the world. Seals and sea lions are expert swimmers, darting through the water looking for fish to eat—or just playing with others. Here's how you can tell them apart.

SEAL	SEA LION

Seals live in family groups.

No outer ears

HARBOR SEAL

Back flippers are fixed and can't be used for walking

Small, finlike front flippers

FAMILY RESEMBLANCE?

Large, footlike front flippers

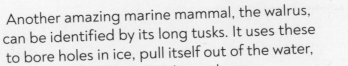

Another amazing marine mammal, the walrus, can be identified by its long tusks. It uses these to bore holes in ice, pull itself out of the water, and fight with other walruses.

NOW YOU KNOW!

These underwater hunters both have chunky bodies and whiskered faces, but sea lions have big flippers that they can use like feet. Along with their ears, these will help you tell them apart from seals.

Small outer ears

Sea lions live in huge groups of up to 1,500 animals, called rafts.

SEA LIONS MAKE BARKING SOUNDS, WHILE SEALS ARE QUIET

CALIFORNIA SEA LION

Back flippers can bend forward for walking on land

FACT FILE

NAME
Harbor seal

WHERE DO THEY LIVE?
Coastlines of the Atlantic and Pacific oceans, and the Baltic and North seas

HOW BIG ARE THEY?
4½–6 ft (1.4–1.8 m) long

WHAT DO THEY EAT?
Fish

NAME
California sea lion

WHERE DO THEY LIVE?
In and around the waters of the west coast of the United States

HOW BIG ARE THEY?
6–7½ ft (1.8–2.2 m) long

WHAT DO THEY EAT?
Fish and squid

EEL OR SEA SNAKE?

What are these creatures winding their way through the ocean? At first glance you might get eels and sea snakes mixed up. Both are long, slender, underwater animals with no limbs. However, if you know what to look for, you'll see that they're very different.

NOW YOU KNOW!

Although they look similar, eels are fish, while snakes are reptiles. Eels have a fishier appearance—with gills and fins—while sea snakes are smoother and shaped more like a cylinder.

EELS CAN BREATHE UNDERWATER THROUGH SLITS IN THEIR BODIES CALLED GILLS

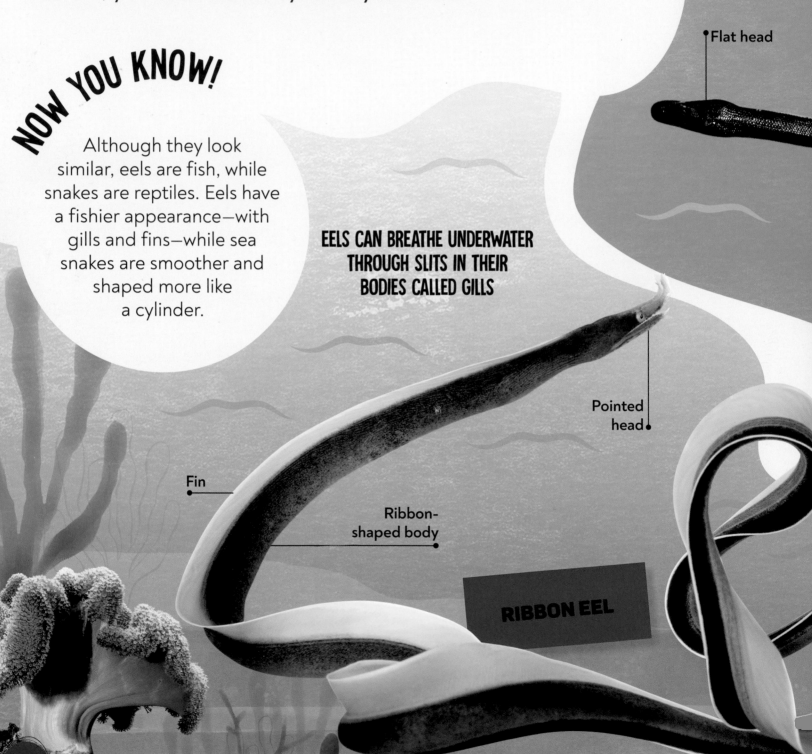

Flat head

Pointed head

Fin

Ribbon-shaped body

RIBBON EEL

FAMILY RESEMBLANCE?

Eels and sea snakes swim by moving their whole bodies in a rolling wave. This movement is called undulation. It is the same way that some snakes, such as cobras, move on land.

EEL　　　**SEA SNAKE**

SOME SEA SNAKES HAVE A HIGHLY VENOMOUS BITE

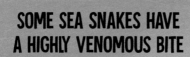

Cylindrical main body with no fins

YELLOW-BELLIED SEA SNAKE

FACT FILE

NAME
Ribbon eel

WHERE DO THEY LIVE?
Coral reefs in the Indian and Pacific oceans

HOW BIG ARE THEY?
35–51 in (90–130 cm) long

WHAT DO THEY EAT?
Fish and shrimp

NAME
Yellow-bellied sea snake

WHERE DO THEY LIVE?
Tropical parts of the Indian and Pacific oceans

HOW BIG ARE THEY?
35 in (90 cm) long

WHAT DO THEY EAT?
Small fish

FLAT FEET
RHINOS HAVE VERY STRONG, FLAT HOOVES THAT SPREAD THEIR WEIGHT OUT OVER THREE TOES TO SUPPORT THEIR HUGE, HEAVY BODIES.

HORSE

RHINOCEROS

HORSE HOOVES
A HORSE'S FOOT IS ACTUALLY ONE BIG TOE WITH ONE BIG TOENAIL! THEY HAVE A SINGLE HOOF ON EACH FOOT, SO THEY CAN RUN ON TOUGH GROUND.

ODD NUMBER OF TOES

There are three different groups of animals that put their weight on one or three of their toes: horses and ponies, tapirs, and rhinoceroses. These groups all have different numbers of toes and hooves.

TAPIR

TAPIR TOES
TAPIRS HAVE FOUR SMALL HOOVES ON THEIR FRONT FEET AND THREE ON THEIR BACK FEET.

Hooves

Hooves protect animals' feet from hot or rocky ground and help them grip onto slippery or icy surfaces. Animals with hooves are sorted into groups, depending on how many toes they put their weight on.

TOUGH SOLES
HIPPOS' HOOVES DO NOT COVER THEIR WHOLE FOOT AND ARE MORE LIKE TOENAILS. HIPPOS HAVE FOUR TOES ON EACH FOOT.

RED DEER

HIPPOPOTAMUS

MINI HOOVES
DEER HAVE "DEW CLAWS"— SMALLER HOOVES TOWARD THE BACK OF THEIR FEET THAT THEY DON'T PUT WEIGHT ON. THESE GIVE THEM EXTRA GRIP.

EVEN NUMBER OF TOES

There are more than 200 different hooved animals that put their weight on two or four toes for standing, walking, or running. This includes pigs, deer, hippopotamuses, and cows.

DEER HAVE TWO MAIN TOES AND TWO DEW CLAWS.

No hooves here!

WHALE

BELIEVE IT OR NOT, DOLPHINS, WHALES, AND PORPOISES ARE IN THE SAME FAMILY AS ANIMALS WITH HOOVES. THIS IS BECAUSE THEIR EARLY RELATIVES HAD HOOVES AND WALKED ON LAND.

AARDVARK OR ANTEATER?

With their long noses and fondness for munching on ants, it's easy to see why people get anteaters and aardvarks mixed up. However, they are actually unrelated animals from different families. How can you tell?

FACT FILE

NAME?
Aardvark

WHERE DO THEY LIVE?
Savannas, grasslands, and woodlands in sub-Saharan Africa

HOW BIG ARE THEY?
14–18 in (36–45 cm) long

WHAT DO THEY EAT?
Ants and termites

NAME
Giant anteater

WHERE DO THEY LIVE?
Central and South America

HOW BIG ARE THEY?
6–8 ft (1.8–2.4 m) long

WHAT DO THEY EAT?
Ants and termites

Light-brown color

Snub, piglike nose

BOTH LIKE TO HUNT AT NIGHT

Claws on front feet

AARDVARK

Cone-shaped tail

Hooves

AARDVARK   ANTEATER

Long,
pointed nose

Paws with
curved claws

FAMILY RESEMBLANCE?

Slow-moving sloths are closely related to anteaters. They both have long claws, but sloths use theirs to hang upside down in trees.

Giant anteaters often have a black stripe along their bodies.

NOW YOU KNOW!

Aardvarks have hooved back legs, while anteaters have four paws. Anteaters have bushy tails and are generally more fluffy than aardvarks, which have short fur.

BOTH HAVE LONG TONGUES FOR SCOOPING UP INSECTS

Bushy tail

GIANT ANTEATER

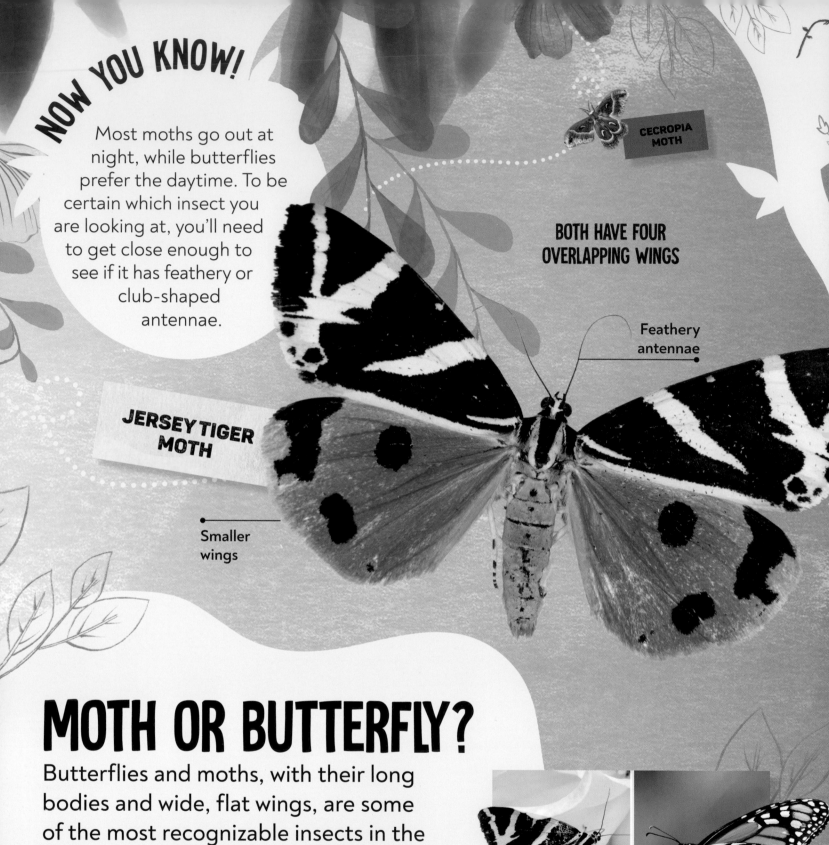

Most moths go out at night, while butterflies prefer the daytime. To be certain which insect you are looking at, you'll need to get close enough to see if it has feathery or club-shaped antennae.

CECROPIA MOTH

BOTH HAVE FOUR OVERLAPPING WINGS

Feathery antennae

JERSEY TIGER MOTH

Smaller wings

MOTH OR BUTTERFLY?

Butterflies and moths, with their long bodies and wide, flat wings, are some of the most recognizable insects in the world. They are important pollinators, helping plants to spread. They are very similar in shape and size, so how can you tell them apart?

MOTH **BUTTERFLY**

JERSEY TIGER CATERPILLAR

FAMILY RESEMBLANCE?

Moths and butterflies start life as eggs, which hatch into caterpillars. To become adults, they go through a process called metamorphosis. Their entire bodies change and they grow wings!

MONARCH CATERPILLAR

BLUE MORPHO BUTTERFLY

Club-shaped antennae

MONARCH BUTTERFLY

Bigger wings

BOTH HAVE LONG, HAIRY BODIES

FACT FILE

NAME
Jersey tiger moth

WHERE DO THEY LIVE?
Gardens and hedgerows in Britain, Eastern Europe, and central Asia

HOW BIG ARE THEY?
2–2½ in (5–6.5 cm) wingspan

WHAT DO THEY EAT?
Nectar from flowers

NAME
Monarch butterfly

WHERE DO THEY LIVE?
Forests and mountains in North and Central America

HOW BIG ARE THEY?
4 in (10 cm) wingspan

WHAT DO THEY EAT?
Milkweed leaves

55

COYOTE OR JACKAL?

There are many wild, doglike animals that belong in the same family as the wolf. Two of these canine cousins, the coyote and the jackal, are very similar, with pointed ears and gray-brown coats. They look almost identical! So what are the differences?

Long, pointed ears

Doglike face

BOTH HAVE YELLOW OR GOLDEN-BROWN EYES

Longer tail

MOUNTAIN COYOTE

COYOTE

JACKAL

The main way to tell whether you're meeting a coyote or a jackal is where you are. If you're in the Americas, it's more likely a coyote, and if you're in Africa or Asia, it's a jackal. Other than that, look closely at their ear and head shapes.

FACT FILE

NAME
Mountain coyote

WHERE DO THEY LIVE?
Deserts, forests, and mountains of North and Central America

HOW BIG ARE THEY?
4 ft (1.1 m) long, of which 11–16 in (30–40 cm) is tail

WHAT DO THEY EAT?
Anything from small mammals, deer, and fish, to insects and fruit

NAME
Golden jackal

WHERE DO THEY LIVE?
Sub-Saharan Africa, South Asia, and parts of Europe

HOW BIG ARE THEY?
27–33 in (69–85 cm) long, of which 9–11 in (20–30 cm) is tail

WHAT DO THEY EAT?
Small animals and birds, plus fruit and vegetables

Pointed, foxlike face

Broad, triangular ears

COYOTES HUNT MOSTLY ON THEIR OWN, WHILE JACKALS WORK IN PAIRS

Shorter tail

GOLDEN JACKAL

FAMILY RESEMBLANCE?

The domesticated dogs that we keep as pets are cousins of coyotes and jackals. Some dogs, such as the German Shepherd (above), still look a bit like their wolf relatives.

PUFFIN OR PENGUIN?

If you take a trip to the coast, you might be lucky enough to come across a colony of funny-looking, black-and-white seabirds. But, depending on where you are, these might be very different birds. Are they puffins or are they penguins?

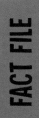

FACT FILE

NAME
Atlantic puffin

WHERE DO THEY LIVE?
Colder areas of the
North Atlantic Ocean

HOW BIG ARE THEY?
11–12 in (28–30 cm) tall, with a
19–25 in (47–63 cm) wingspan

WHAT DO THEY EAT?
Mostly fish, but also shrimp,
shellfish, and worms

NAME
Emperor penguin

WHERE DO THEY LIVE?
Antarctica

HOW BIG ARE THEY?
3½–4 ft (1.1–1.2 m) tall

WHAT DO THEY EAT?
Fish, squid, and shellfish

**BOTH LIVE IN HUGE
COLONIES WITH HUNDREDS
OF OTHER BIRDS**

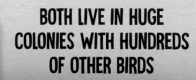

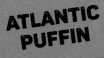
ATLANTIC
PUFFIN

Chunky,
colorful beak

Short
wings

Small,
round body

NOW YOU KNOW!

The biggest difference between these two birds is flight—if it's flying, it's definitely a puffin. The puffin's short, blunt, orange-and-yellow beak is another giveaway.

PUFFIN

PENGUIN

Long, pointed beak

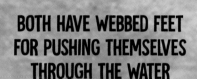

EMPEROR PENGUIN

BOTH HAVE WEBBED FEET FOR PUSHING THEMSELVES THROUGH THE WATER

Stiff flippers for swimming

Long body

FAMILY RESEMBLANCE?

Because they live in and around the water, seabirds such as puffins, penguins, and razorbills (right) have special oily, waterproof feathers.

REPTILES

Many reptiles can see more colors than we can see, while snakes' eyes can detect heat.

LEAF VIPER

NO EYELIDS NEEDED
SNAKES DON'T HAVE EYELIDS, JUST A THIN LAYER OF SKIN OVER THEIR EYES, CALLED A SPECTACLE.

LICKING LIZARD

Some lizards don't have eyelids. Instead of blinking to keep their eyes moist, they lick their eyeballs!

ON THE HUNT
THE FORWARD-FACING EYES OF PREDATORS SUCH AS FOXES HELP THEM TELL HOW CLOSE OR FAR AWAY SOMETHING IS, WHICH MAKES IT EASIER TO CATCH PREY.

FOX

MAMMALS

You can often tell whether a mammal is a predator or prey by looking at its eyes. Prey animals usually have their eyes at the sides of their heads, while predators usually have forward-facing eyes.

BLACK-TAILED JACKRABBIT

KEEPING WATCH
EYES ON THE SIDES OF THEIR HEADS HELP PREY ANIMALS SEE A WIDE AREA AROUND THEM, SO THEY CAN SPOT DANGER.

Eyes

Nearly every animal has eyes, but eyes are very different, depending on what they are used for. Does the animal need to see in the dark, look behind it, or spot tiny things far away?

INSECT EYES
FLIES HAVE LARGE EYES MADE UP OF THOUSANDS OF TINY INDIVIDUAL EYES! THEY CAN SEE COLORS WE CAN'T SEE.

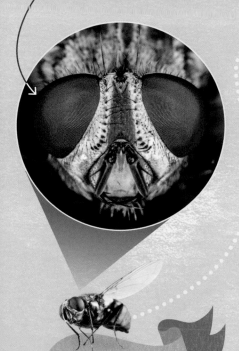

FLY

NIGHT VISION
If an animal has very big eyes, it's probably because it needs to see in the dark. A nighttime animal, such as an owl, often has a mirrorlike area behind its eyes that absorbs even tiny amounts of light.

LOOK AROUND
UNLIKE MOST ANIMALS, OWLS CAN'T MOVE THEIR EYES. INSTEAD, THEY ROTATE THEIR HEADS NEARLY ALL THE WAY AROUND SO THEY CAN SEE WHAT'S GOING ON BEHIND THEM.

URAL OWL

MANY LEGS, MANY EYES
SPIDERS ARE HUNTERS. THEY HAVE MANY EYES TO HELP THEM SPOT THEIR PREY.

INSECTS & SPIDERS
The eyes of creatures without a backbone, such as insects, are very different from the eyes of mammals and birds. Insects have hundreds or thousands of tiny eyes that can see in all directions.

JUMPING SPIDER

WINGSPOTS
SOME MOTHS AND BUTTERFLIES HAVE DEVELOPED SPOTS ON THEIR WINGS THAT LOOK JUST LIKE STARING PREDATOR EYES. THESE HELP TO FRIGHTEN OFF ANY POTENTIAL ATTACKERS.

These eyes can't see!

SEAGULL

ALBATROSS

BOTH HAVE WHITE AND
DARK-GRAY FEATHERS

Large
wings

EUROPEAN
HERRING GULL

Heavy, slightly
hooked beak

Hind toe
on foot

SEAGULL OR ALBATROSS?

Seagulls and albatrosses are both large seabirds with
a clear pattern of white and gray feathers. They can
both be seen soaring above the ocean, occasionally
dropping down under the waves to snatch a fish.
How can you tell these two big, marine birds apart?

NOW YOU KNOW!

Seagulls tend to live on coasts, where they can scavenge for food, while albatrosses spend most of their lives in the air and at sea. Albatrosses are much, much bigger!

NAME
European herring gull

WHERE DO THEY LIVE?
Coasts in Western Europe

HOW BIG ARE THEY?
24–26 in (60–67 cm) long, with a 4–5 ft (1.2–1.5 m) wingspan

WHAT DO THEY EAT?
All sorts, from fish to human garbage and sewage

NAME
Short-tailed albatross

WHERE DO THEY LIVE?
North Pacific Ocean

HOW BIG ARE THEY?
33–37 in (84–94 cm) long, with a 6¾–7½ ft (2.1–2.3 m) wingspan

WHAT DO THEY EAT?
Fish, fish eggs, and shellfish

Massive wingspan

Long, hooked beak

BOTH HAVE WEBBED FEET FOR WATERY LANDINGS

SHORT-TAILED ALBATROSS

No hind toe

FAMILY RESEMBLANCE?

Gannets are also seabirds, with white feathers, black wingtips, long necks, and long, pointed beaks. They can be seen diving gracefully into the water for food.

TORTOISE OR TURTLE?

All tortoises are actually part of the turtle family—although not all turtles are tortoises! When we talk about turtles, we mean the ones that live in the sea. So, how do you tell the difference between these hard-shelled reptiles?

GALÁPAGOS GIANT TORTOISE

Domed, heavy shell

Chunky legs

FACT FILE

NAME
Galápagos giant tortoise

WHERE DO THEY LIVE
The Galápagos Islands, off the coast of Ecuador

HOW BIG ARE THEY?
Up to 4 ft (130 cm) long

WHAT DO THEY EAT?
Grass, leaves, and cacti

NAME
Hawksbill sea turtle

WHERE DO THEY LIVE?
Tropical coral reefs in the Atlantic and Pacific oceans

HOW BIG ARE THEY?
2–3 ft (60–95 cm) long

WHAT DO THEY EAT?
Sea sponges, along with algae, sea plants, and small fish and mollusks

TORTOISES ARE VEGETARIAN, WHILE TURTLES EAT BOTH PLANTS AND ANIMALS

FAMILY RESEMBLANCE?

Terrapins are turtles that live in lakes and ponds. They can swim, but they have feet like tortoises and spend part of their time on land.

Galápagos giant tortoises can live to more than 150 years old.

TORTOISE

TURTLE

NOW YOU KNOW!

Tortoises live on land, while turtles live in the sea. Look to see if they have feet or flippers, and at the shape of their shells, for clues about whether they walk or swim.

Turtles return to the beach where they were born to lay their eggs.

Flipperlike legs

HAWKSBILL SEA TURTLE

Light, streamlined shell

BOTH HAVE A HARD BEAK AND SCALY SKIN

65

HEDGEHOG OR PORCUPINE?

If you see either of these spiked creatures, be careful! They both use their spikes, called quills, to protect themselves from predators. They both also like to come out at night. Can you tell them apart?

FACT FILE

NAME
European hedgehog

WHERE DO THEY LIVE?
Woodlands and gardens across western Europe

HOW BIG ARE THEY?
6–12 in (15–30 cm)

WHAT DO THEY EAT?
Insects, eggs, and worms

NAME
Indian crested porcupine

WHERE DO THEY LIVE?
Forests in western and central Asia

HOW BIG ARE THEY?
27–35 in (70–90 cm) long, with a 3–4 in (8–10 cm) tail

WHAT DO THEY EAT?
Fruit, berries, roots, and bark

HEDGEHOGS HAVE AROUND 7,000 QUILLS

Short quills that don't fall out

Small, round body

Pointed nose

EUROPEAN HEDGEHOG

HEDGEHOG

PORCUPINE

Hedgehog quills are short, so the hedgehog protects itself by rolling into a spiked ball. Porcupine quills are longer and fall out easily, so the spikes get stuck in an attacker's skin.

PORCUPINES HAVE AROUND 30,000 QUILLS

Long quills that fall out

Bigger body

Rounded nose

INDIAN CRESTED PORCUPINE

FAMILY RESEMBLANCE?

Even though it has no quills, the common shrew's pointed nose is a clue that it's related to the hedgehog.

DAMSELFLY OR DRAGONFLY?

These slender, colorful insects are a common sight near ponds and lakes, especially in the summer. They live near still water, preying on smaller flying insects. Damselflies and dragonflies look so similar that many people think they're the same thing—but we know better.

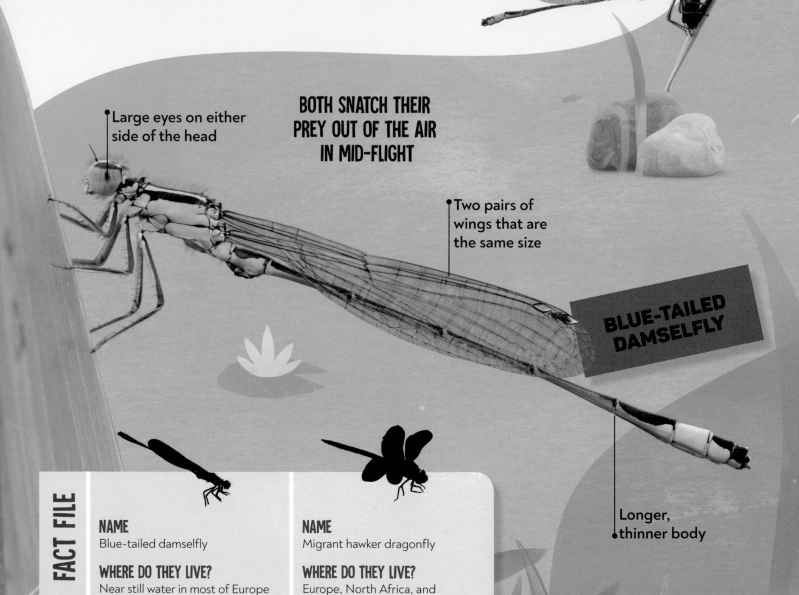

Large eyes on either side of the head

BOTH SNATCH THEIR PREY OUT OF THE AIR IN MID-FLIGHT

Two pairs of wings that are the same size

BLUE-TAILED DAMSELFLY

Longer, thinner body

FACT FILE

NAME
Blue-tailed damselfly

WHERE DO THEY LIVE?
Near still water in most of Europe

HOW BIG ARE THEY?
1 in (3 cm) long, with 1½ in (3.5 cm) wingspan

WHAT DO THEY EAT?
Small flying insects and insect larvae (young)

NAME
Migrant hawker dragonfly

WHERE DO THEY LIVE?
Europe, North Africa, and across Asia, including Japan

HOW BIG ARE THEY?
2½ in (6.5 cm) long, with 3 in (8 cm) wingspan

WHAT DO THEY EAT?
Small flying insects

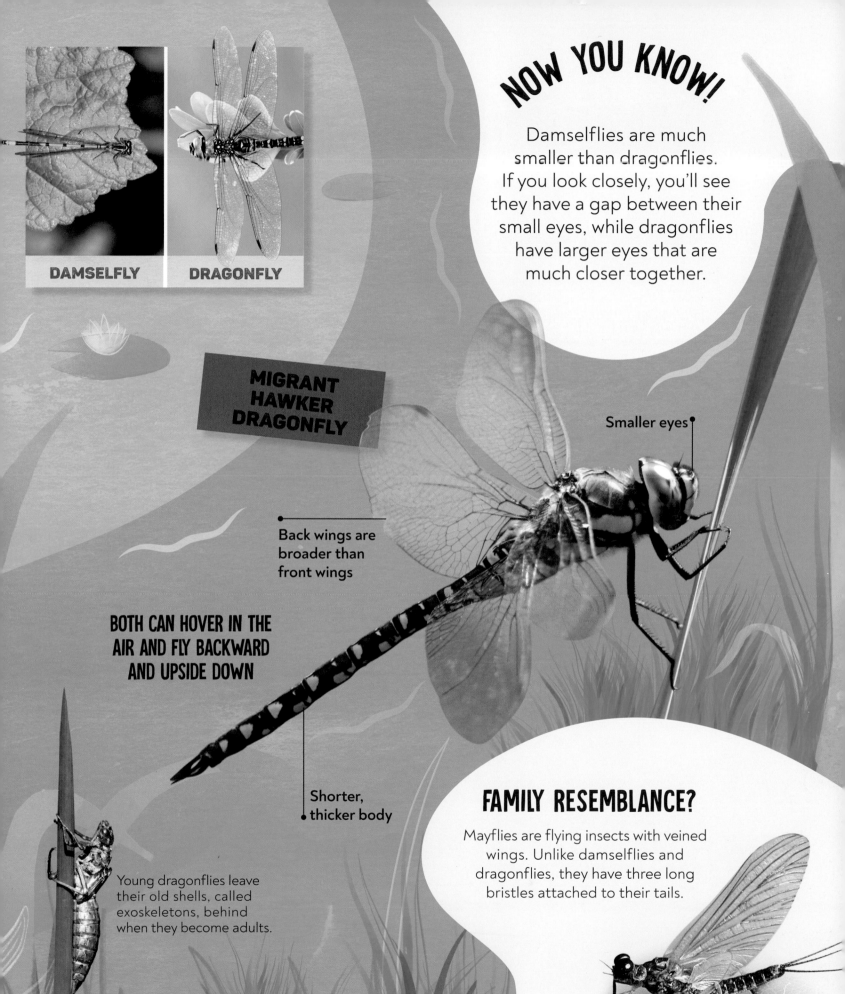

DAMSELFLY

DRAGONFLY

Damselflies are much smaller than dragonflies. If you look closely, you'll see they have a gap between their small eyes, while dragonflies have larger eyes that are much closer together.

MIGRANT HAWKER DRAGONFLY

Smaller eyes

Back wings are broader than front wings

BOTH CAN HOVER IN THE AIR AND FLY BACKWARD AND UPSIDE DOWN

Shorter, thicker body

FAMILY RESEMBLANCE?

Mayflies are flying insects with veined wings. Unlike damselflies and dragonflies, they have three long bristles attached to their tails.

Young dragonflies leave their old shells, called exoskeletons, behind when they become adults.

COZY CORAL
CANDY CRABS SIT ON CORALS THE SAME COLOR AS THEY ARE, AND EVEN WEAR CORALS TO HELP THEM BLEND IN.

CANDY CRAB

BROWN BARK
THE FEATHERS OF EASTERN SCREECH OWLS ARE ALMOST IDENTICAL TO THE BARK OF THE TREES WHERE THEY PERCH.

BLENDING IN
Many animals are a similar color and pattern to the environment where they live, making them hard to spot.

TIGER

STRIPED PREDATOR
THIN STRIPES MAKE TIGERS HARD TO SPOT AMONG THE TALL GRASSES WHERE THEY STALK PREY.

CHAMELEON

ALL CHANGE
CHAMELEONS CAN CHANGE THE COLOR AND PATTERN OF THEIR SKIN TO MATCH THEIR SURROUNDINGS.

Camouflage
Some animals need to hide from predators to protect themselves from being eaten. Others want to sneak up on their prey. Camouflage helps keep animals from being noticed.

CORAL SNAKE

MILK SNAKE

DEADLY OR SAFE?
CORAL SNAKES HAVE A VENOMOUS BITE. MILK SNAKES HAVE NO VENOM, BUT THEIR COLORS AND STRIPES LOOK SO MUCH LIKE CORAL SNAKES' THAT PREDATORS ARE SCARED OFF.

ORCHID MANTIS

FLOWER OR MANTIS?
ORCHID MANTISES LOOK ALMOST EXACTLY LIKE PINK ORCHIDS. THE MANTISES SPEND THEIR DAYS PERCHED ON THESE FLOWERS AND ARE ALMOST IMPOSSIBLE TO SPOT.

MIMICS

Animals without much protection against predators can use camouflage to mimic another creature. This means they look like something else, often a dangerous or poisonous animal that predators would not want to bother.

MOTH OR SPIDER?
METALMARK MOTHS HAVE PATTERNS ON THEIR BACKS THAT LOOK LIKE JUMPING SPIDER EYES. THIS CONFUSES ANY SPIDERS THAT ARE HUNTING THEM.

METALMARK MOTH

Stay together!

STANDING OUT

ZEBRAS' STRIPES MAKE IT DIFFICULT FOR A SINGLE ZEBRA TO BE PICKED OUT OF A HERD. THIS MEANS THAT IT IS A HARDER TARGET FOR PREDATORS, SUCH AS LIONS.

STORK OR HERON?

Herons and storks are tall, long-necked birds that live in and around water. They can both be found standing very still in ponds, watching the surface for snacks. But which of these stately birds is which?

STORK

HERON

Thick bill that curves at the top

Short, straight neck

BOTH HAVE VERY SHARP BEAKS THAT CAN SPEAR FISH

MARABOU STORK

NOW YOU KNOW!

A stork's bill curves at the top, while a heron's is flatter. If you spot one of these birds in flight, you'll see that a stork flies with its neck stretched out, while a heron's neck forms a clear "S" shape.

NAME
Marabou stork

WHERE DO THEY LIVE?
All kinds of habitats in sub-Saharan Africa, from savannas to swamps

HOW BIG ARE THEY?
60 in (152 cm) tall

WHAT DO THEY EAT?
Fish, frogs, garbage, rotting meat, and poop

NAME
Great blue heron

WHERE DO THEY LIVE?
Wetlands of North and Central America

HOW BIG ARE THEY?
36–54 in (91–137 cm) tall

WHAT DO THEY EAT?
Small fish

Smaller, pointed bill

S-shaped neck

Herons build their nests high up in the trees.

GREAT BLUE HERON

BOTH HAVE LONG LEGS SO THEY CAN WADE IN DEEP WATER

FAMILY RESEMBLANCE?

Another long-legged water bird, the crane is famous for its elaborate dances. The sandhill crane (above) is easy to identify because of its red "hat."

SEA OTTER OR RIVER OTTER?

These two animals are closely related. Both are excellent swimmers with playful natures. However, living in the sea is very different from living along the banks of a river. Let's find out how to tell these cute creatures apart.

SEA OTTER   **RIVER OTTER**

Ears are almost invisible

Sea otters can spend their whole lives in the water. Their babies have waterproof fur, which helps them float.

SEA OTTER

Thick, fluffy fur

FAMILY RESEMBLANCE?

Otters are part of the weasel family, which also includes badgers and stoats. The weasel (below) is a fierce hunter that can take down animals bigger than itself.

SEA OTTERS LOVE TO FLOAT ON THEIR BACKS, WHILE RIVER OTTERS ONLY SWIM ON THEIR FRONTS

NAME
Sea otter

WHERE DO THEY LIVE?
Coasts of the North
Pacific Ocean

HOW BIG ARE THEY?
4–5 ft (1.2–1.5 m) long

WHAT DO THEY EAT?
A wide range of prey, including
sea urchins, crustaceans, snails,
and octopuses

NAME
North American river otter

WHERE DO THEY LIVE?
Rivers and marshes in Canada
and the United States

HOW BIG ARE THEY?
26–42 in (66–107 cm) long

WHAT DO THEY EAT?
Fish, crayfish, small reptiles and
amphibians, birds, and even
larger animals, such as beavers
and snapping turtles

River otters spend
most of their time
on land.

SEA OTTERS CAN DIVE 100 FT (30 M) UNDERWATER, WHILE RIVER OTTERS CAN DIVE 60 FT (18 M)

Short,
coarse fur

Round,
tapered tail

All four feet are
a similar size

Visible ears

NORTH AMERICAN
RIVER OTTER

Pawlike front feet
and flipperlike
back feet

Broad,
flat tail

NOW YOU KNOW!

Sea otters are much,
much bigger than river
otters, sometimes weighing
up to nine times as much. In
addition to that, sea otters have
thicker fur, giving them a
fluffier appearance.

GLOSSARY

AMPHIBIAN
Type of animal that lives both in water and on land

ANTENNAE
Pair of long, thin feelers on the head of an insect

BILL
Bird's beak

CAMOUFLAGE
Way in which an animal blends into the background to avoid being seen

CANINE
Member of the dog family. Also describes doglike features

CANINE TOOTH
Pointed, sharp tooth near the front of an animal's mouth

CARNIVORE
Animal that eats only meat

CETACEANS
Group of mammals that live in the sea. Includes dolphins, porpoises, and whales

COARSE
Rough in texture

COLD-BLOODED
Describes an animal whose body cools down or warms up according to its surroundings

EXOSKELETON
Hard shell that some invertebrates have

FRESHWATER
Water that is not salty. Includes rivers, lakes, and ponds

GLIDING
Flying without flapping wings

HABITAT
Home environment of an animal, plant, or other living thing, including the natural features, such as water and rocks, that make up the surroundings

HEMISPHERE
Half of the Earth. The Southern Hemisphere includes South America, Africa, Australasia, and Antarctica. The Northern Hemisphere includes North America, Europe, Asia, and the Arctic

HERBIVORE
Animal that eats only plants

HYBRID
Animal or plant that is a mix of two different, closely related species

INCISORS
Teeth at the front of some animals' mouths, used for biting into food

INSECT
Type of small invertebrate with six legs

INVERTEBRATE
Animal without a backbone, such as an insect, octopus, or squid

LARVA
Young of an insect

LITTER
Group of baby animals born at the same time to the same mother

MAMMAL
Warm-blooded, often hairy type of animal that mostly gives birth to young rather than laying eggs

MARSUPIAL
Type of animal with a pouch, where its babies spend part of their lives

METAMORPHOSIS
When an animal goes through a major change to its body. For example, when a larva turns into an adult insect or a tadpole becomes an adult frog

MIMICKING
Describes an animal copying another animal

MOLARS
Teeth at the back of a mammal's mouth that are used to grind down food

NOCTURNAL
Describes an animal that is mostly active at night

OMNIVORE
Animal that eats both meat and plants

PEST
Animal that damages food supplies or crops

PINCER
Large claw of a crab

POLLINATOR
Insect or other animal that spreads pollen from one plant to another so that it can grow fruit

PREDATOR
Animal that hunts and eats other animals

PREHENSILE
Describes an animal's limb, often a tail, that is flexible and can be used to grasp branches

PREMOLAR
Tooth between the front teeth and the broader, flatter molars at the back of an animal's mouth

PREY
Animal that is hunted and eaten by a predator

QUILL
Sharp spike that grows out of the skin of hedgehogs, porcupines, and some other mammals

RAPTOR
Bird of prey, such as a falcon, hawk, or eagle

REPTILE
Type of cold-blooded animal with scaly skin

SALTWATER
Type of water with a lot of salt in it, such as the sea

SAVANNA
Flat, dry, grassland habitat

SCAVENGER
Animal that feeds on dead and rotting animals and plants

SEABIRD
Bird that lives and hunts for food in or near the sea

SNOUT
Long nose of an animal

SPECIES
Group of animals that have the same features. Animals of the same or closely related species can have young together

TALON
Sharp claw of a bird of prey

TENTACLE
Long, thin limb of some underwater invertebrates, such as squid. Tentacles have suckers along them and are used to grab food and feel things

TOXIN
Poison created in the bodies of plants or animals, such as poison dart frogs

VENOM
Poison that an animal inserts into the skin of its victim when it bites or stings them

WATERFOWL
Birds that live and feed in water

WINGSPAN
Distance between the wing tips of a bird or other flying animal

WINGTIPS
Ends of a bird's wings

INDEX

ACKNOWLEDGMENTS

DK would like to thank: Kritika Gupta for editorial assistance; Nehal Verma for design support; Dheeraj Arora for jacket design support; Mayank Choudhary for additional picture research; Polly Goodman for proofreading; and Helen Peters for the index.

PICTURE CREDITS

The publisher would like to thank the following for their kind permission to reproduce their photographs: (Key: a-above; b-below/bottom; c-center; f-far; l-left; r-right; t-top)

1 Dreamstime.com: Birute Vijeikiene (cl). **Shutterstock.com:** Milan Vachal (cr). **2–3 Alamy Stock Photo:** George Ostertag (cb). **Dreamstime.com:** Alexandrebes (tc). **2 Alamy Stock Photo:** Zoonar / Knut Niehus (br). **Dreamstime.com:** Xiebiyun (cl). **3 Alamy Stock Photo:** Frank Hecker (b). **Dreamstime.com:** Allexxandar (tr/Mallard); Thomas Marx (tr). **4 Dreamstime.com:** Stuartan (bl). **Getty Images / iStock:** Trifonov Evgeniy (cra). **4–5 Dreamstime.com:** Jody Overstreet (bc). **5 Getty Images / iStock:** Antagain (cla); Gerald Corsi (tr). **6 Dreamstime.com:** Edwin Butter (br); Volodymyr Kucherenko (tl); Steve Byland / Stevebyland (tc). **Getty Images / iStock:** OldFulica (bl). **7 Alamy Stock Photo:** Shane Gross / Nature Picture Library (cr); Jelger Herder / Buiten-beeld / Minden Pictures (bl). **Getty Images:** Chóng Shàng Zhi / EyeEm (tr); Kevin Schafer (tl). **8 Alamy Stock Photo:** Andrew DuBois (cra); CORDIER Sylvain / hemis.fr (bl). **Getty Images / iStock:** Abstract Aerial Art (br); imageBROKER / Harry Laub (bc). **naturepl.com:** Visuals Unlimited (c). **8–9 Dreamstime.com:** Scottbrownphoto2012 (ca). **9 Alamy Stock Photo:** George Grall (cr). **Dreamstime.com:** Hakoar (b); Mariana Ionita (tc). **10 Alamy Stock Photo:** Richard Tadman (cb). **Dreamstime.com:** Dmitriyrnd (cr, cra, tr); Isselee (cl); Iakov Filimonov (ca). **11 Alamy Stock Photo:** Richard Tadman (tr, c, clb). **Dreamstime.com:** Bigjohn3650 (crb); Meunierd (tl); Lars Ove Jonsson (tc); Isselee (ca); Rudolf Ernst (ca/Vicunas); Fotorince (cr). **12 Dreamstime.com:** Adeliepenguin (tl); Yodke67 (cl); Dennis Schaefer (c). **Getty Images / iStock:** Raimund Linke (cr). **13 Alamy Stock Photo:** Guillermo Lopez Barrera (clb); Joe McDonald / Steve Bloom Images (cl); Will Burrard-Lucas / Nature Picture Library (cra, tr); Stephen Dalton / Nature Picture Library (crb). **Dreamstime.com:** Agami Photo Agency (cla); Malcolmarouza (c); Jan Martin Will (bl). **14 Alamy Stock Photo:** blickwinkel / McPHOTO / A. Schauhuber (tr); Clarence Holmes Wildlife (bc). **Dreamstime.com:** Ulrike Leone (br); Nenad Nedomacki (cla); Birute Vijeikiene (c). **15 123RF.com:** alekss (tc/Ladybugs). **Dreamstime.com:** Dmitry2016911 (c); Hakoar (tl); Isselee (tr, ca/Firebug). **Getty Images / iStock:** gawrav (ca). **Shutterstock.com:** Milan Vachal (tc, b). **16 Dreamstime.com:** Alexandrebes (c); Bill Kennedy (bc); Veronika Preobrazhenskay (br). **Getty Images:** Chóng Shàng Zhi / EyeEm (tl). **17 Alamy Stock Photo:** Bill Coster (cra/Racoon); Frank Hecker (b). **Dreamstime.com:** Coconutdreams (cra). **Getty Images:** Kevin Schafer (ca). naturepl.com: Aflo (cr). **18 Alamy Stock Photo:** Genevieve Vallee (bc). **Getty Images:** Wild Horizons / Universal Images Group (cra). **19 Alamy Stock Photo:** dpa picture alliance archive (b, cr); Andrey Nekrasov (ca/octopus). **Getty Images:** Wild Horizons / Universal Images Group (ca). **Shutterstock.com:** Yusran Abdul Rahman (c). **20 Dreamstime.com:** Dragoneye (cr); Isselee (cra). **Getty Images / iStock:** JohnCarnemolla (c). **21 Dreamstime.com:** Agami Photo Agency (br); Khunaspix (l); Robert Downer (tc); Thepoo (tc/Ostrich foot); Fullempty (cr). **22 Alamy Stock Photo:** Tom Gilks (tc). **Dreamstime.com:** Peter Etchells (cl); Isselee (c). **Getty Images / iStock:** Coprid (b). **Getty Images:** Vicki Jauron, Babylon and Beyond Photography (tr). **23 Dreamstime.com:** Slowmotiongli (cla). **Getty Images / iStock:** Coprid (tc). **naturepl.com:** Klein & Hubert (b). **Shutterstock.com:** Kalidron.Photography (tr). **24 Alamy Stock Photo:** Mike Parry / Minden Pictures (tr). **Science Photo Library:** George D. Lepp (cl). **24–25 Dreamstime.com:** Sergey Uryadnikov (c). **25 123RF.com:** Andrei Samkov / satirus (bl). **Alamy Stock Photo:** Clement Philippe / Arterra Picture Library (cr). **Getty Images:** DeAgostini (tl); Ed Reschke (cra). **26 Alamy Stock Photo:** chris24 (br); Gerry Pearce (cl); Roland Seitre / Minden Pictures (bl). **Dreamstime.com:** Marc Witte (ca). **Getty Images:** Morey Milbradt (cra). **27 Dreamstime.com:** Holly Kuchera (cl). **naturepl.com:** Steve Gettle (b). **28 Alamy Stock Photo:** Barrett & MacKay / All Canada Photos (tc); Wild Wonders of Europe / Campbell / Nature Picture Library (tl); Radius Images / Design Pics (cra). **Getty Images / iStock:** Michel VIARD (ca). **28–29 Alamy Stock Photo:** Shane Gross / Nature Picture Library (c). **29 123RF.com:** Simone Gatterwe / gatterwe (br). **Alamy Stock Photo:** Jelger Herder / Buiten-beeld / Minden Pictures (cb). **Getty Images / iStock:** Gerald Corsi (ca). **30 123RF.com:** Daniel Prudek (Bee). **Dreamstime.com:** Melinda Fawver (cra); Johan007 (bc); Henrikhl (ca); Verastuchelova (cra/Leaf); Stuartan (cr). **Getty Images / iStock:** Oqvector (l). **31 Alamy Stock Photo:** Ron Erwin / All Canada Photos (clb). **Dreamstime.com:** Adamdudzik (br); Johan007 (cl); Maciej Olszewski (cr). **Getty Images / iStock:** Antagain (cla/Flying); Trifonov Evgeniy (cla/Wasps). **32 Alamy Stock Photo:** Sylvain Cordier / Biosphoto (tr). **Dreamstime.com:** Helen Davies (ca, tc); Brian Lasenby (ca/Pika). **33 Alamy Stock Photo:** FLPA (tr, c); Ron McCombe (cr). **34 Alamy Stock Photo:** Christina Krutz / agefotostock (ca); Werner Layer / mauritius images GmbH (tc); George Ostertag (c); Zoonar / Knut Niehus (cr). **Dreamstime.com:** Karelgallas (tl). **35 Dreamstime.com:** Allexxandar (c); Darius Strazdas (bl). **Getty Images / iStock:** NatalyaAksenova (ca). **36 Alamy Stock Photo:** De Meester Johan / Arterra Picture Library (l). **Getty Images / iStock:** Michael Warren (tr). **36–37 Getty Images / iStock:** CDH_Design (bc). **37 Alamy Stock Photo:** Nature Picture Library (cb); WaterFrame_dpr (br). **Dreamstime.com:** Isselee (cl); Jmrocek (tl); Zina Seletskaya (cra). **38 Alamy Stock Photo:** André Gilden. **Dreamstime.com:** Appfind (cb); Waldemar Manfred Seehagen (crb). **39 Alamy Stock Photo:** Jeff Foott / Nature Picture Library (c). **Dreamstime.com:** Isselee (br); Andrian Muhamad Yusup (tr); Sous (b). **40 Alamy Stock Photo:** Arndt Sven-Erik / Arterra Picture Library (cb); Joao Ponces (crb). **Getty Images / iStock:** VladGans (c). **41 Dreamstime.com:** Isselee (bl); Wannasak Saetia (cra); Natallia Yaumenenka (crb). **42 123RF.com:** battle182royal (tc/Leaves). **Dreamstime.com:** Isselee (tr); Suchanon Sukjam (tr/leaf); Taviphoto (tc). **Getty Images / iStock:** AlasdairJames (cr). **43 123RF.com:** Jennifer Barrow / jenifoto (c/sand). **Alamy Stock Photo:** Chris Mattison (c). **Dreamstime.com:** Jpldesigns (tc/Lily Pads); Cristian M. Vela (br). **Getty Images / iStock:** AlasdairJames (tc). **44 Dreamstime.com:** Jan Hejda (crb); Volodymyr Kucherenko (c); Mikelane45 (cb). **Shutterstock.com:** Mark Medcalf (tr). **45 Dreamstime.com:** Richard Lowthian (bc); Steve Byland / Stevebyland (c); Jay Pierstorff (tr, crb). **Getty Images:** Gary Chalker (cb). **46 Alamy Stock Photo:** David Tipling Photo Library (c); Harry M. Walker / Alaska Stock / Design Pics Inc (cla); Russell Millner (tc). **Dreamstime.com:** Susanne Neal (tr). **Getty Images / iStock:** Gerald Corsi (bl). **47 Alamy Stock Photo:** CBpictures / Westend61 GmbH (ca). **Getty Images / iStock:** Stephanie Kenner (b). **48 Dreamstime.com:** Isselee (b). **Getty Images:** Giordano Cipriani (bl). **49 Alamy Stock Photo:** Pete Oxford / Minden Pictures (c); Underwater Imaging (tl). **Dreamstime.com:** Johnpierpont (tc). **Getty Images / iStock:** sunstock (tc/Cobra). **50 Dreamstime.com:** Feverpitched (tc); Karin Van Ijzendoorn / Satara910 (tl); Maria Itina (cl); Pavel Naumov (tr). **Shutterstock.com:** Picsoftheday (cb). **50–51 Dreamstime.com:** Wrangel (cb). **51 Alamy Stock Photo:** Arndt Sven-Erik / Arterra Picture Library (cb); Karen van der Zijden (br). **Dreamstime.com:** Friedemeier (tl); Isselee (cr). **52 Alamy Stock Photo:** Martin Harvey (fcra). **Dorling Kindersley:** Lynette Schimming (cra). **Getty Images:** Life On White (br). **53 Dreamstime.com:** Lukas Blazek (tc); Isselee (cr). **Getty Images / iStock:** KenCanning (tr). **Getty Images:** wendy salisbury photography (tl). **54 123RF.com:** Geza Farkas (cr). **Alamy Stock Photo:** Colin Varndell (bc). **Dreamstime.com:** K Quinn Ferris (br); Jason Ondreicka (tr). **55 Dreamstime.com:** Cathy Keifer (ca); Thawats (c). **Getty Images / iStock:** LPETTET (tr). **Shutterstock.com:** Eileen Kumpf (tl). **56 Dreamstime.com:** Jmrocek (cb); Jay Pierstorff (cl); Denis Pepin (clb). **Getty Images / iStock:** OldFulica (br). **57 Dreamstime.com:** Edwin Butter (bl); Isselee (crb). **58 Dreamstime.com:** Holgers (b/Puffin); Spolcycstudio (b); Pisit Rapitpunt (cra). **59 Alamy Stock Photo:** World Travel Collection (cra). **Dreamstime.com:** Gentoomultimedia (tr); Hakoar (tc); Rudmer Zwerver (br). **Getty Images / iStock:** VargaJones (c). **60 Dreamstime.com:** Isselee (cl). **Getty Images / iStock:** Mark Kostich (cla); Kaan Sezer (cra); rancho_runner (crb). **61 Dorling Kindersley:** Natural History Museum, London (bl, br). **Dreamstime.com:** Razvan Cornel Constantin (cb); Rene Alberto Mayorga Villarreal (cla); Michael Biehler / Gewoldi (cl). **Getty Images / iStock:** efcarlos (crb); KaidoKarner (cra). **62 Alamy Stock Photo:** Tui De Roy / Minden Pictures (tc/Short-tailed Albatross); Arndt, S.-E. / juniors@wildlife (tr). **Dreamstime.com:** Tupungato (tc). **naturepl.com:** Nick Upton (c). **63 Alamy Stock Photo:** Tui De Roy / Minden Pictures. **Dreamstime.com:** Verastuchelova (bc). **64 123RF.com:** Chonlasub Woravichan (clb). **Dorling Kindersley:** Twan Leenders (bc). **65 123RF.com:** Chonlasub Woravichan. **Alamy Stock Photo:** Karol Kozlowski / imageBROKER (tc/Galápagos giant tortoise). **Dreamstime.com:** Lirtlon (cr); Engdao Wichitpunya (cra); Shakeelmsm (cra/hatching). **Getty Images / iStock:** Delves Photography (tc). **Shutterstock.com:** Rich Carey (tr). **66 Dreamstime.com:** Isselee (fclb, cla, crb, tr); Konstantin Nikiteev (clb); Pstedrak (cra). **67 Alamy Stock Photo:** VPC Animals Photo (c). **Dreamstime.com:** Cynoclub (tc/house); Ondřej Prosický (tl); Rudolf Ernst (tc); Isselee (tc/European hedgehog); Rudmer Zwerver (br). **68 Dreamstime.com:** Marekkijevsky (c, clb, cra); Sandra Standbridge (cb). **69 Alamy Stock Photo:** Lee Beel (tc). **Dorling Kindersley:** Melvin Grey (br). **Dreamstime.com:** Ottovanrooy (tl); Sandra Standbridge (c). **Getty Images / iStock:** pixelleo (bl). **70 Dreamstime.com:** Yashvardhan Dalmia (cl); Wirestock (tr); Tsu Shi Wong (cr). **Getty Images / iStock:** Laurasiy (cla). **71 Alamy Stock Photo:** Colin Marshall / agefotostock (c). **Dreamstime.com:** Slowmotiongli (ca). **Getty Images / iStock:** cinoby (br). **Shutterstock.com:** Coulanges (cla); Jamikorn Sooktaramorn (tr). **72 Alamy Stock Photo:** Ilukee (cl); Christopher Scott (clb). **Dreamstime.com:** Martin Maritz (c). **Getty Images / iStock:** irvingnsaperstein (r). **73 Dreamstime.com:** Rinus Baak (cr); Charles Brutlag (cl). **Shutterstock.com:** Danita Delimont (crb). **74 Alamy Stock Photo:** Brian Gibbs (bl); Milo Burcham / Design Pics Inc (cl); Thomas Kitchin & Victoria Hurst / Design Pics Inc (tc). **Dreamstime.com:** Mirkorosenau (tr); Jody Overstreet (br). **75 Alamy Stock Photo:** Konrad Wothe / Minden Pictures (c). **Dreamstime.com:** (tl). **Getty Images / iStock:** Gerald Corsi (tr). **77 Dreamstime.com:** Isselee (b). **Getty Images / iStock:** LPETTET (crb). **78 Alamy Stock Photo:** Tui De Roy / Minden Pictures (tc). **79 Dreamstime.com:** Jan Martin Will (br). **80 Alamy Stock Photo:** WaterFrame_dpr (br). **Getty Images / iStock:** KaidoKarner (tl).

COVER CREDITS *Front:* **123RF.com:** Anton Starikov clb; **Dreamstime.com:** Volodymyr Byrdyak c, Hakoar br, Murbanska00 cr, Julian Peters cl, Tratong c/ (Jaguar); *Back:* **123RF.com:** Igor Dmitriev / kotomiti cra, Isselee Eric Philippe cla; **Alamy Stock Photo:** Nature Picture Library cr; **Dreamstime.com:** Isselee bl, bc, Alexander Potapov cl; *Spine:* **123RF.com:** Geza Farkas cb/ (Tiger moth); **Dreamstime.com:** Melinda Fawver cb/ (Wasp), Daniel Prudek cb, Thawats bc

All other images © Dorling Kindersley